life FOUNDATIONS

GOD'S LOVE FOR YOU

It's Not Your Love for God

CARRIE PICKETT

Dedication

This book is dedicated to my mom, Karen Nordquist, my first teacher. An amazing Sunday school teacher, she always included God's love in every lesson. Those lessons became my foundation.

To Mike, my husband, who reflects God's love to me in the kindest, deepest, and most consistent ways. Your love has transformed me.

To my babies, Elliana and Michael. On the days you were born, I held you in awe and experienced a deeper revelation of God's love the moment I first held you. To believe that God loves us even more than I loved you the first time I saw you... wow.

And to Jesus—above all else, I dedicate this book to You, because You first loved me. Thank You, dearest Savior, for showing me every day how much You love me. Oh, to experience the greater width, depth, height, and breadth of Your love—I am ready.

Published by Andrew Wommack Ministries, Inc.

Woodland Park, CO 80863

ISBN 13 TP: 978-1-6675-1545-8

ISBN 13 eBook: 978-1- 6675-1546-5

For Worldwide Distribution, Printed in the USA

1 2 3 4 5 6 / 29 28 27 26

Table of Contents

Foreword

The Bible says we love God because He first loved us (1 John 4:19). Yet so much ministry today is all about how we are supposed to love God. Our love for God can only come as the result of a true revelation of His love for us. We can't give what we haven't received.

There are many great attributes about Carrie, but I believe everyone who knows her would put her emphasis on God's love for us at the top of the list. She models it in a powerful way, and it is always woven into everything she teaches.

I've known Carrie since she was ten years old. I used to minister at her church in Kit Carson, Colorado. She came to Charis Bible College when she was just 19, and upon graduation, she went to Russia as a missionary for sixteen years. This was at the beginning of our ministry, and we didn't give her anything but our love, a prayer, and a pat on the back. She was a single young woman who went on a shoestring budget to start a Bible school above the Arctic Circle. It was a baptism by fire, and she not only survived but thrived.

It was in Russia that she met her husband, Mike, who was also a missionary there. They ran our Charis Bible College with extension campuses all over Russia. They translated my books and put my program on TV across the Russian-speaking world. They proved themselves faithful and more than competent. They have touched the lives of millions of people.

They came back to Colorado in 2014 for a little break, and the Lord spoke to me that they could reach more people from our home base than if they were out on the field. Although they loved being on the mission field, they began to take on more and more leadership here, and today, they are the ones the Lord has designated to take over Charis Bible College and Andrew Wommack Ministries as I get older. I can't give them any higher recommendation than that.

First John 4:8 and 16 say that God is love. Love is a person, and His love was expressed by giving His Son to take our place and receive our punishment. Jesus didn't do this when we had our act together. He gave His love to us while we were still sinners (Rom. 5:8). Now that we have accepted His forgiveness, He loves us even more (Rom. 5:9-10). Understanding God's unconditional love for us is the key to operating in faith (Gal. 5:6).

It does no good to believe God is able if we can't get past our feelings of unworthiness. We must uncouple God's love from our performance. The Lord loves us because He is Love, not because we are lovely. Carrie does an awesome job of explaining this. We've heard many testimonies from our Charis students about how Carrie's class on the love of God changed their lives. I believe it will change yours too.

Andrew Wommack

Introduction

You know, I think one of the biggest misunderstandings in the Christian walk is the idea that we're the ones doing all the pursuing. That we have to chase God down, work hard to find Him, earn His love, and somehow keep ourselves from messing it all up. But the truth is—God has always been the One pursuing us.

This book, *God's Love for You*, is not about trying to love God better. It's not a checklist of how to be more spiritual. It's not a motivational guide for self-improvement. It's a revelation. A journey into discovering a love that is far deeper, wider, and stronger than we've ever imagined. A love that doesn't back off when we struggle. A love that doesn't stop when we fall short. A love that doesn't slow down when we feel lost. No, this love runs after us—relentlessly.

Whether you've walked with the Lord for decades or you're just beginning to discover who He really is, this book is for you. It's for the ones who have tried hard and still feel empty. It's for the ones who feel like they've failed too many times. It's for the ones who are hungry for more but don't know how to get there. And it's for the ones who've started to wonder if maybe they're just not enough.

Over the course of these chapters, we're going to unpack what it means to be fully known and fully loved by God. We'll dive into the Word and explore what His promises say about your identity, your healing, your authority, and your destiny. We'll expose the lies of religion and fear, and instead, plant you firmly in the truth of grace and relationship. You'll hear real stories, walk through powerful Scripture, and be invited—again and again—into the embrace of a God who is not distant, disappointed, or disinterested. He is close, He is present, and He is pursuing you.

My prayer is that as you turn these pages, your heart awakens to just how personal this love is. That you won't just believe God loves people—you'll believe He loves you. And not the cleaned-up, got-it-all-together version of you—the real you. The one He created. The one He redeemed. The one He delights in.

So, get ready to be reminded of what's always been true.
Get ready to exchange shame for peace. To trade fear for faith.
To step into your identity with boldness.
To walk in healing, power, and purpose. Because the pursuit is not over. It's only just beginning.

And the One who is pursuing you...
He's relentless.

Chapter One

The Movement of God

The God Who Moves Toward Us

I have loved the Lord since I was a young girl, and I'm so excited to share this word that He has put on my heart. There is something so powerful about the love of God—it is not just an emotion or a passive feeling. The love of God is movement. It is action. It is a force that pursues, redeems, and transforms.

For years, I have witnessed the movement of God first-hand—both in my own life and the lives of people around the world. As a missionary in Russia, I saw people who had been bound by religious traditions, believing that God's love was conditional. But when they encountered the truth of God's love, it changed everything.

That is why this message is so important. The enemy has tried to twist and pervert the love of God, making it seem like it is something we have to earn. But the truth is that God's love is not dependent on us—it is entirely based on Him. He is the One who moves toward us, not the other way around.

So, as we walk through this chapter together, grab a cup of coffee, open your heart, and allow the Word of God to show you just how much He loves you.

God's Movement Begins with Love

John 3:16 says, "*For God so loved the world that He gave His only begotten Son, that whoever believes in Him should not perish but have everlasting life*" (*New King James Version*).

Notice the movement in that verse—God *so loved* that He *gave*. God didn't wait for us to be perfect. He didn't wait for us to reach out to Him. He *moved first*. This is what sets God's love apart from human love. Human love often comes with conditions: *I love you if...* or *I love you when...* But God's love is different. He doesn't love us based on what we do for Him—He loves us because of who He is.

The enemy wants us to believe that we must earn God's love through our actions—through how much we give, how often we serve, or how long we pray. But that is a lie. If we had to earn His love, then it would not be grace—it would be a wage. But God's love is freely given.

God's Movement is in Pursuit of the Lost

Matthew 18:11-12 says, "*For the Son of Man has come to save that which was lost. What do you think? If a man has a hundred sheep, and one of them goes astray, does he not leave the ninety-nine and go to the mountains to seek the one that is straying?*" (*NKJV*).

God does not wait for us to find Him—He comes after us. He seeks us out when we are lost. He pursues us, not out of obligation, but out of love.

I have seen this so clearly in my years of ministry. I remember one particular moment during a minister's conference in a Russian village. We were teaching on the love of God, and it felt like plowing through rock. The people had been taught that God was a harsh dictator, demanding perfection. For three days, we just kept speaking the Word, praying, believing that the truth would break through, and it did. Many lives were changed when they realized that the love of God—His active, pursuing movement—is towards them. He doesn't just save us—He brings us into the full knowledge of His love.

How God Draws Us In

Romans 2:4 says, "*Or do you despise the riches of His goodness, forbearance, and longsuffering, not knowing that the goodness of God leads you to repentance?*" (NKJV).

Many people have been taught that repentance is about fear—that if we don't repent, God will punish us. But the Bible tells us something completely different. It says that it is God's goodness that leads us to repentance. It is His kindness, patience, and incredible love that draw us back to Him.

I have met so many believers who feel like they have to be perfect before they can come to God. They believe that if they have sinned, they must first clean themselves up before they can pray, read the Word, or even go to church. But this is exactly the kind of deception that keeps people in bondage.

God does not stand at a distance, arms crossed, waiting for us to get our act together. No! He runs toward us. He meets us in our brokenness and draws us in with His love. His goodness is what softens our hearts and turns us back to Him.

Think about the prodigal son in Luke 15. The son had squandered everything, and yet the father didn't wait for him to apologize perfectly or prove that he had changed. The moment the father saw his son from afar, he ran to him, embraced him, and restored him. That's the heart of God toward us!

Repentance is not about fear of punishment—it is about responding to love. When we understand the goodness of God, we no longer run from Him—we run to Him.

How the Cross Reconciled Us to God

Romans 8:32 says, "*He who did not spare His own Son, but delivered Him up for us all, how shall He not with Him also freely give us all things?*" (*NKJV*).

The cross is the greatest demonstration of God's movement toward us. God's love is not passive. He didn't just say, "I love you." He showed it by giving His Son. The sacrifice of Jesus was not simply about our salvation for eternity; it was about reconciling us to the heart of the Father, bringing us into relationship with Him now.

This love is so powerful that it changes everything. It takes us from being slaves to sin and makes us children of God. It removes the barriers between us and the Father. And if God was willing to give us His Son, why would He withhold anything else that we need? His love is not just about eternity—it is about life now, about walking in His fullness and receiving His blessings.

Nothing Can Separate Us from the Movement of God's Love

Romans 8:35-39 says, "*Who shall separate us from the love of Christ? Shall tribulation, or distress, or persecution, or famine, or nakedness, or peril, or sword? As it is written: "For Your sake we are killed all day long; we are accounted as sheep for the slaughter." Yet in all these things we are more than conquerors through Him who loved us. For I am persuaded that neither death nor life, nor angels nor principalities nor powers, nor things present nor things to come, nor height nor depth, nor any other created thing, shall be able to separate us from the love of God which is in Christ Jesus our Lord*" (*NKJV*).

No trial, no hardship, no failure, no attack of the enemy—nothing—can separate us from the love of God. The enemy constantly whispers lies to make us feel disqualified. He tells us that our mistakes, our past, or even our current struggles make us unworthy of God's love. But that is a complete deception.

God's love is based on His pursuit, not our perfection. That means He does not stop loving us when we struggle. He does not turn His back when we fail. He does not withhold His presence until we "get it together." His love remains constant, and nothing can change that.

This is why the enemy fights so hard to distort the truth of God's love—because once we truly understand it, we become unshakable. We stop living in fear and insecurity. We stop striving to earn love that has already been freely given. We stand firm, knowing that we are deeply loved by the Creator of the universe, and nothing can separate us from Him.

If we could grasp the width, depth, and height of God's love, we would walk in absolute confidence and peace. No longer would we be tossed about by doubts and lies. Instead, we would boldly declare, "I am more than a conqueror through Him who loves me."

No matter what you are going through today, know this: God's love is not fragile. It does not fade. It does not weaken. It is strong, unrelenting, and eternal. Nothing—absolutely nothing—can separate you from it.

God's Love Empowers Us to Live in Victory

Romans 5:5-8 says, "*Now hope does not disappoint, because the love of God has been poured out in our hearts by the Holy Spirit who was given to us. For when we were still without strength, in due time Christ died for the ungodly. For scarcely for a righteous man will one die; yet perhaps for a good man someone would even dare to die. But God demonstrates His own love toward us, in that while we were still sinners, Christ died for us*" (NKJV).

James 1:21-22 reinforces this truth, saying, "*Therefore lay aside all filthiness and overflow of wickedness, and receive with meekness the implanted word, which is able to save your souls. But be doers of the word, and not hearers only, deceiving yourselves*" (NKJV).

The love of God is not just a comforting thought—it is a force that empowers us. It is not merely a concept to be studied or a doctrine to be recited; it is a reality that strengthens us to live in victory. Knowing we are loved helps us stand against the lies of the enemy. The enemy works tirelessly to make us feel weak, inadequate, and unworthy. But when we are rooted in God's love, we stand firm, unshaken by circumstances.

This is not an attitude of obligation but of faith and victory. We don't serve God out of guilt; we serve Him from a place of confidence, knowing that we are deeply loved. We don't pray to earn His favor; we pray because we have already received His favor through Christ.

When we allow His love to shape our identity, we walk in boldness, knowing that no matter what comes our way, we are already victorious through Him. His love gives us the courage to step out in faith, the endurance to persevere through trials, and the assurance that we are never alone.

So, when trials arise, we can boldly declare: *I am victorious because I am loved. I stand firm because I am loved. I overcome because I am loved.* This revelation changes everything—it shifts our perspective, strengthens our faith, and leads us into the abundant life Christ has promised.

The Love of God is Demonstrated in Action

Hebrews 9:24 and 26 says, "*For Christ has not entered the holy places made with hands,* which *are copies of the true, but into heaven itself, now to appear in the presence of God for us; ... now, once at the end of the ages, He has appeared to put away sin by the sacrifice of Himself*" (*NKJV*).

First John 4:9-10 says, "*In this the love of God was manifested toward us, that God has sent His only begotten Son into the world, that we might live through Him. In this is love, not that we loved God, but that He loved us and sent His Son* to be *the propitiation for our sins*" (*NKJV*).

God moves toward us with love, and that love takes action. His love is not just a statement—it is demonstrated. Jesus did not remain distant, waiting for us to come to Him. Instead, He took on flesh, walked among us, and became the sacrifice for our sins.

He *appeared before God for us* to be our advocate. The high priest of the Old Testament would enter the Holy of Holies once a year, bringing a sacrifice for the sins of the people. But Jesus, our eternal High Priest, entered not an earthly temple but the very presence of God—on our behalf. He didn't just say He loved us; He demonstrated it through His sacrifice.

This is the difference between human love and divine love. People can say they love, but true love is proven in action. Jesus proved His love with every step toward the cross, with every lash He bore, with every drop of blood He shed. Love was not just His message—it was His mission.

When we grasp this truth, it changes everything. We are no longer striving to earn love but responding to love already given. We don't serve God out of fear—we serve because we are overwhelmed by His goodness. And as we receive that love, we become vessels of it, allowing His love to move through us and impact those around us.

God's love is active. It pursues. It saves. It transforms. And when we live in the revelation of that love, we don't just hear the truth—we *become* the truth in action.

Receiving the Movement of God's Love

Titus 3:5 says, "*Not by works of righteousness which we have done, but according to His mercy He saved us, through the washing of regeneration and renewing of the Holy Spirit*" (NKJV).

Second Corinthians 5:17 says, "*Therefore, if anyone* is *in Christ,* he is *a new creation; old things have passed away; behold, all things have become new*" (NKJV).

The only qualification for receiving God's love is to be human. Christ did not come for the righteous—He came for sinners. Many people feel they aren't worthy of God's love. They look at their past, their mistakes, and their failures, and believe they are disqualified. But the truth is that God made the first move. He didn't wait for us to be worthy—He came while we were still sinners. His love is based on who He is, not on what we have or haven't done.

Once we receive His love, everything changes. We stop striving. We stop trying to earn His acceptance. Instead, we start living from His love rather than for it. There is a huge difference between striving for God's love and simply receiving it. When we receive it, we rest in the assurance that we are fully accepted, fully forgiven, and fully loved.

God's love is not something we work for—it is something we live from. When we understand this, our relationship with God transforms from one of duty and obligation to one of joy and freedom. We no longer live under the burden of performance; we walk in the abundance of His grace.

If you have ever felt unworthy, I want to encourage you today: God's love is already yours. You don't have to qualify for it. You don't have to prove yourself. You simply have to receive it. And once you do, you will step into the fullness of everything He has for you.

A Life Transformed by the Movement of God

One of the greatest testimonies I have personally witnessed about the transformational power of God's love came from a pastor in Russia. This woman had been in ministry for twenty years, faithfully preaching the Gospel and serving her congregation. Yet, despite all those years of ministry, she had never fully grasped the reality that God truly loved her.

She had known about God's power, His commands, and His righteousness, but the idea that He loved her personally, unconditionally, and completely had never sunk in. She had spent decades striving—working hard for God, laboring under a mindset that she had to prove her devotion through service and sacrifice. The message of God's love was foreign to her, just as it was to so many others who had grown up under a harsh, condemning view of God.

During one of our ministers' conferences in a small Russian village, we taught on the love of God—not as an obligation, not as something to be earned, but as a gift freely given. The atmosphere was heavy at first. Years of religious tradition had ingrained in these believers that God's love was something they had to strive for. It was as if we were breaking through solid rock with every verse we shared.

But then, on the third day, something changed. This pastor—this faithful servant of God—came up to us in tears. She finally saw it.

"I finally see that God loves me," she said. "I've been preaching for twenty years, and I never knew."

I remember standing there, my heart overflowing with joy and sorrow at the same time. Joy, because I knew this revelation was going to transform her life forever. Sorrow, because I thought, *What have you been preaching for the last twenty years if you never knew that God loved you?*

But this is the reality for so many believers. They serve, they pray, they try to be "good enough," but they never fully receive the love of God for themselves. They hear about His power, His commands, His expectations—but they miss His heart.

That moment changed everything for her. When she finally saw the movement of God's love—that He initiated the pursuit, that He had been chasing after her all along—it set her free. It shifted her from legalism to relationship. She no longer saw her service as something that earned her place with God. Now, she served from a place of love, not striving.

This is what happens when we receive the revelation of God's love—it changes everything.

The enemy wants to keep us bound in a mindset of performance-based faith, where we constantly feel we have to do more to be accepted by God. But the love of God frees us from that burden. It moves us from obligation to intimacy. It takes us from legalism to relationship.

The movement of God's love doesn't just rescue us from sin—it reshapes the way we live our lives. When we know we are loved, completely and unconditionally, we stop striving. We stop performing for God's approval. We stop trying to earn what has already been freely given. Instead, we start living in His love, moving in His grace, and responding to His goodness.

If God's love could transform a pastor after twenty years of ministry, how much more can it transform you today?

The question is not whether God is moving toward you—the question is whether you will receive that love.

His love is already in motion. He has already made the first move. The only thing left is for you to say, *Yes, Lord, I receive it.*

Final Thoughts: Embracing the Movement of God's Love

God's love is not based on performance—He has already moved toward us through Jesus Christ. He made the first move, not because we earned it, but because He is love. His love is constant, unshaken by our failures, unwavering in the face of our weaknesses, and enduring through every season of our lives.

When we embrace His unconditional love, we begin to walk in confidence, faith, and boldness. We no longer live from a place of striving or fear, but from assurance and rest. Instead of trying to prove our worth, we live from the reality that we are already deeply loved and fully accepted.

No matter what has happened in your past, no matter how many mistakes you have made or how many times you have felt unworthy, God is saying to you today:

"I love you."

"I pursue you."

"Nothing can separate you from My love."

The movement of God's love is an invitation—to step into relationship over religion, to embrace grace over works, and to receive His love as the foundation of your life. When you understand that His love is not something you have to strive for, but rather something you can rest in, everything changes.

This revelation leads to freedom. It leads to transformation. It allows you to stand firm, knowing that you are secure in the hands of your Heavenly Father. The enemy will try to convince you that you have disqualified yourself. But here's the truth: God's love for you has never wavered, and it never will.

Call to Action:

Let the love of God be the foundation of your life and step into the abundant life He has for you!

Scriptures Referenced

- John 3:16
- Matthew 18:11-13
- Romans 2:4
- Romans 8:32, 35-39
- Titus 3:5
- Romans 5:5-8

- Hebrews 9:24, 26
- 1 John 4:9-10
- James 1:21-22
- 2 Corinthians 5:17

Chapter Two

Deeper Revelation

A Love That Never Stops Pursuing

The love of God is not a one-time lesson but an ongoing revelation that deepens as we grow in our walk with Him. It is the very heartbeat of God towards us, constantly drawing us closer. Whether we have just begun our journey with the Lord or have walked with Him for years, there is always more—more power, more life, and more depth in His love than we have ever realized before.

When I started teaching and preaching, I was a young girl. I remember being in Bible school at Charis, and one of my teachers said, "You need to find your life message." And I thought, *what's a life message?* He said, "It's something that's so deep in your heart, you wouldn't need your Bible to share it—you could be woken up in the middle of the night, and that message would flow out of you." And I thought, *Lord, what is my life message?* And it was during Bible school that I started to get a revelation—not just that I was saved, not just that I was called—but that I was loved.

I had grown up in a church that taught the finished work of the cross, the righteousness we have in Christ, and the power of grace. But even though I knew these things intellectually, it wasn't until Bible school that all those truths truly came together. They were meant to form a real relationship with God, not just a theological foundation. That's when I understood: many people settle for an intellectual knowledge of God's love rather than experiencing it.

Experiencing God's Love Beyond Knowledge

Many people know about God's love, but few truly experience it. There is a difference between knowing something intellectually and living in the reality of it. I have met so many believers who can quote scripture about God's love but struggle to actually feel loved by Him. They believe God loves them in theory, but in their daily lives, they operate as if they must still earn His favor.

We are not meant to just read about God's love—we are called to walk in it, to let it permeate every part of who we are. This is why 1 John 4:9-10 is so powerful: "*In this was manifested the love of God toward us: that God has sent His only begotten Son into the world, that we might live through Him. Herein is love: not that we loved God, but that He loved us and sent His Son to be the propitiation for our sins*" (*21st Century King James Version*). God's love is not based on our ability to love Him back. He loved us first. That means even in our lowest moments, His love remains constant.

Changed By Divine Love

The love of God can transform anything you let it touch. Anything. Your marriage, your finances, your health, your self-worth. When you let the love of God touch an area of your life, it changes. I have seen it over and over again.

Second Corinthians 5:17 says, "*Therefore, if anyone is in Christ, he is a new creation. The old has passed away; behold, the new has come*" (*English Standard Version*).

That means your past is completely erased by His love. But the enemy will always try to remind you of it. He'll bring up your mistakes, your failures. And sometimes, people will, too. You'll hear voices saying, "Remember when you failed? Remember that mistake?" But God is saying, "I've made you new."

I have had the privilege of working with people coming out of drug addiction and prison, people who believed their past defined them. But when they encountered the love of God, they became unrecognizable. One young woman came to Bible school straight out of prison, and within months, she was radiant with joy. That's the power of His love.

The Prodigal Son: A Story of Love

One of the greatest illustrations of God's love is found in the story of the prodigal son (Luke 15:11-24). This parable is such a beautiful, rich example of God's heart towards us. It's not just a story about a rebellious son—it's about the overwhelming, relentless love of the Father.

I grew up on a farm, and I know what it's like to feed pigs. It's messy. It stinks. You don't leave a pig pen without carrying the smell of it with you. The prodigal son wasn't just physically in a bad place—he was covered in shame, regret, and the consequences of his decisions. He had squandered everything, lost all his so-called friends, and was now left feeding pigs. For a Jewish man, there was nothing lower than being among the pigs. This was rock bottom.

And yet, it says in Luke 15:17, "*When he came to himself, he said, 'How many of my father's hired servants have more than enough bread, but I perish here with hunger!'*" (*ESV*). That's the moment of revelation. He realized that even his father's servants were treated better than this. But here's what's key—he didn't yet understand the depth of his father's love. He was still thinking in terms of earning a place. He planned to return, not as a son, but as a servant. He rehearsed his speech: "*Father, I have sinned against heaven and before you. I am no longer worthy to be called your son. Treat me as one of your hired servants*" (Luke 15:18-19, *ESV*).

But here's the beauty of God's love: The father never intended for him to return as a servant. He was always a son. And the moment the father saw him, "*while he was still a long way off, his father saw him and felt compassion, and ran and embraced him and kissed him*" (Luke 15:20, *ESV*).

I love that! The father wasn't waiting at the house, arms crossed, tapping his foot, saying, "Let's see if he's really sorry." No! He was watching, looking, anticipating his return. And when he saw him, he ran. He ran! In that culture, men of dignity didn't run. Running meant lifting your robe, exposing your legs, which was considered shameful. But the father didn't care. His love was too great to hold back.

I imagine the son must have been shocked. He was expecting rejection, or at best, a cold reception. But instead, before he could even finish his rehearsed apology, his father interrupted him, embraced him, and restored him. "*Bring quickly the best robe, and put it on him, and put a ring on his hand, and shoes on his feet*" (Luke 15:22, *ESV*).

Do you see what's happening? The father wasn't just welcoming him home—he was restoring his identity. The robe covered his filth. The ring represented authority and sonship. The shoes meant he was not a servant—servants didn't wear shoes. Every detail in this moment shouts the overwhelming, restoring, redemptive love of God.

I think of how many times in my own life I've had moments of failure and regret, moments where I felt like I had to clean myself up before coming back to God. But that's not how He operates. He meets us in our mess, wraps us in His love, and says, "You were always mine."

And here's the truth—some of us have a prodigal past, but all of us have had a prodigal heart at some point. We've all had times where we ran from God, where we chose our own way, where we thought we had messed up too much. But God is always looking, always waiting, always ready to run toward us the moment we turn back to Him.

The father's love in this story is radical, scandalous even. The older brother in the story didn't understand it. He was offended that the father would celebrate the return of someone who had squandered so much. But that's the thing about God's love—it offends the self-righteous. It makes no sense to the world. It is lavish, reckless, and completely undeserved. And yet, it's ours.

This story isn't just about the prodigal son. It's about the love of the Father. It's about you and me. It's about all of us who have wandered, who have doubted, who have believed the lie that we had to earn our way back. And it's about the truth that we never stopped being His.

The Indwelling of God's Spirit

The love of God is not just an abstract concept—it is a living, active force that resides within us. When we receive Jesus, we don't just receive forgiveness; we receive Him. The Spirit of God Himself comes to live inside of us. Romans 8:9-11 reminds us, "*You, however, are not in the flesh but in the Spirit, if in fact the Spirit of God dwells in you. ... If the Spirit of him who raised Jesus from the dead dwells in you, he who raised Christ Jesus from the dead will also give life to your mortal bodies*" (*ESV*). That same power that raised Jesus from the dead is alive in us today.

I love how Andrew Wommack describes it: "When we want to talk to God, we don't look up there. We look down here at our chest, our own body." Because He is not far away, waiting for us to earn His attention—He is within us! That means His love is not something we are trying to reach for, but something we already possess. The person of love dwells within us, and that changes everything.

When we grasp this truth, it transforms the way we live. We don't have to strive to love others in our own strength. When we face difficult people or painful situations, we can love them with the love of God, which is already inside of us. How many times have we said, "I just can't love them, I just don't have it in me"? But the truth is, we do! Not because of our own efforts, but because love Himself dwells in us.

I have seen people in the worst circumstances—broken relationships, deep betrayals, overwhelming loss—find the strength to forgive and love again, not because they mustered it up, but because they tapped into the love that was already inside of them. When we lean into the Spirit of God within us, we stop striving and start walking in the fullness of His love.

This is why we can have confidence, even in the midst of trials. God's love is not something we earn—it is something we live from. And because He dwells in us, we are never without His presence, His power, or His love.

Romans 8:9-11 reminds us that the same Spirit that raised Christ from the dead now lives in us. That means His power, His authority, and His love are dwelling inside of us. We don't have to beg God for His love or try to earn it. He has already placed His love within us by His Spirit.

The Sovereignty of God and His Goodness

God's love is not a controlling force that manipulates circumstances for His own amusement. His sovereignty does not mean that He causes bad things to happen in our lives. Jeremiah 31:3 says, "*Yes, I have loved you with an everlasting love; Therefore with lovingkindness I have drawn you*" (*NKJV*). His goodness draws us, not hardship.

One of the greatest lies the enemy tries to get people to believe is that God is responsible for their pain. Some people have been taught that sickness, loss, or hardship are "lessons" from God, a way for Him to draw them closer or to make them better Christians. But that's not the nature of a loving Father. The devil has twisted the truth of God's sovereignty to make people passive in their suffering instead of resisting the enemy's attacks.

I remember sitting with people who were broken—people who had lost children, people struggling with disease, people who had been told by well-meaning Christians that "God must have a reason" for their suffering. I wanted to shake them and say, "No! That's not my God!" Our God is a healer, a restorer, a redeemer. He does not use, nor does He need, the tools of the enemy to discipline His children. If we don't understand this, we won't resist the attacks of the enemy—we'll accept them, thinking they're part of God's mysterious will.

Jesus made the nature of God clear when He walked on the earth. He healed the sick, He set the captives free, He provided for the needy. He never once said, "You need to stay sick a little longer so you can learn something." No! Jesus responded the way the Father would. Jesus said in John 14:9, "*He who has seen Me has seen the Father*" (*NKJV*). That means if we want to know what God is like, we just have to look at Jesus. Everything Jesus did—healing, delivering, saving—was an expression of the Father's heart.

Some people say, "Well, what about the trials I've been through? I've grown closer to God through them." And yes, there are people who, in their darkest moments, have turned to God and experienced deep intimacy with Him. But here's the key—God didn't cause the darkness. He met you there. He didn't send the storm, but He walked with you through it. And if you had sought Him before the storm, you would have found Him just as near.

James 4:7 tells us, "*Resist the devil, and he will flee from you*" (*ESV*). That means we need to be able to distinguish what is from God and what is from the enemy. If we mistakenly believe that every hardship, sickness, and tragedy is from God, we won't resist it. We won't fight back. But when we know the truth, we rise up with the authority given to us as His children and declare, "No! This is not from my Father! This is an attack of the enemy, and I will not accept it!"

God's sovereignty does not mean He is distant and uninvolved. It means He is above all things, and in His sovereignty, He gave us authority on this earth. He loves us enough to work through us, not to control us like puppets. He has already given us His Spirit, His promises, and His power—now He calls us to walk in them. Understanding this changes our approach to and view of God. We stop blaming God for our struggles and start partnering with Him to walk in victory.

Walking in Our New Identity

When we come into a revelation of God's love, it transforms how we see ourselves. We no longer identify with who we used to be—we now identify with who we are in Christ. First John 3:1 declares, "*See what kind of love the Father has given to us, that we should be called children of God; and so, we are*" (*ESV*). This is not just a title—it is our new reality.

For so many years, people have struggled with defining themselves by their past—by their failures, their sins, or what others have said about them. The enemy works overtime to keep us tied to an old identity, constantly reminding us of our worst moments. But God is constantly speaking a different reality over us: "You are mine. You are loved. You are righteous." When we truly receive this revelation, it breaks the chains of shame and self-doubt.

I remember working with men in a drug rehabilitation center. They were coming out of years of addiction, abusive relationships, and crime. They saw themselves as addicts, as failures, as people beyond redemption. But when they began to understand the love of God—when they saw that He wasn't standing over them in condemnation but was instead running toward them with open arms—it changed them. I saw them go from brokenness to wholeness, from hopelessness to joy. The moment they received that they were loved, that they were righteous in Christ, their entire demeanor shifted. They walked taller. They spoke differently. They believed that they were new creations in Christ, and they lived like it.

Remember, 2 Corinthians 5:17 says, "*Therefore, if anyone is in Christ, he is a new creation. The old has passed away; behold, the new has come*" (*ESV*). This is not just a hopeful idea—it is the truth. When God looks at us, He doesn't see the mistakes of our past. He sees His righteousness in us. He sees us through the lens of Christ's finished work. That means we don't have to live under condemnation, guilt, or the weight of our old failures.

But here's the key—we have to walk in this new identity. If we don't actively renew our minds with the truth of who we are, the enemy will try to pull us back into old mindsets. He'll whisper, "You haven't really changed. You're still the same person. You're still a failure." But that's a lie. Romans 8:9-11 reminds us that the same Spirit that raised Jesus from the dead now lives in us. That means we have the power to live as new creations—not by striving, but by allowing His Spirit to work in us.

The world may not recognize our transformation. First John 3:1 says, "*The reason why the world does not know us is that it did not know him*" (*ESV*). People who knew us before may still see us through the lens of our past. They may remind us of who we used to be. But that doesn't change who we are now. Our identity is not based on what others say—it is based on what God has declared.

I have had moments where I felt the weight of my own insecurities. Moments where I doubted if I was really walking in everything God had called me to. But every time, God reminded me, "You are not defined by your past. You are defined by My love." That's the message I want you to receive today. You are not who you used to be. You are loved. You are redeemed. You are a child of God.

Look again at 1 John 3:1, which declares, "*See what kind of love the Father has given to us, that we should be called children of God; and so we are*" (*ESV*). Understanding God's love means knowing that we are His children. We no longer have to live under the identity of our past.

The Overflow of Relationship with God

Many believers wrestle with understanding their calling, thinking that it is something distant or difficult to uncover.

But our primary calling is not found in what we do—it is found in knowing Him. Everything else flows from that relationship. When we cultivate intimacy with God, the overflow of that relationship reveals our gifts, our talents, and our purpose. We were not created to chase after a calling—we were created to chase after Him, and in doing so, everything else falls into place.

I remember struggling with this myself. I wanted to know exactly what I was supposed to do for God. I wanted to have a clear direction, a specific purpose mapped out before me. But God spoke to my heart, "You are called to Me first. Everything else will come from that." And I realized something powerful—when we allow ourselves to be loved by God, everything in our lives begins to align with His plans.

When we live in the overflow of His love, we don't walk in fear of failure. We stop striving for approval. We stop comparing ourselves to others, wondering if we are doing enough. We rest in the assurance that He has called us into relationship, not just service. The beauty of this is that as we grow in intimacy with Him, we naturally begin to walk in His promises. We start to declare with boldness, "Healing is mine, provision is mine, my children belong to the Lord." Not because we are striving, but because we know who we are.

I have seen this transformation in others as well. Students in Bible school who came searching for a grand calling suddenly found peace when they stopped focusing on what they were supposed to do and started focusing on who they were in Christ. And from that place of relationship, ministry began to flow effortlessly. They began to lead, to teach, to walk in boldness—not because they had a five-step plan for success, but because they had surrendered to the love of God and let it guide them.

God does not want us to live stressed and confused about our future. He wants us to rest in His love and let that relationship produce the overflow. Just as Jesus said in John 15:5, "*I am the vine; you are the branches. If you remain in me and I in you, you will bear much fruit; apart from me you can do nothing*" (*New International Version*). When we remain in Him, fruit is inevitable. The overflow of our relationship with God will touch every area of our lives, allowing us to walk in our calling with confidence and joy.

Many struggle with knowing their calling, but our primary calling is to know Him. Out of that intimacy, our overflow—our gifts, talents, and purpose—becomes evident. When we allow ourselves to be loved by God, we begin to walk in His promises, declaring, "Healing is mine, provision is mine, my children belong to the Lord."

Final Thoughts: Encountering Deeper Revelation

Understanding the depth of God's love changes everything. His love is not meant to be a distant concept but a living, breathing reality in our lives. It calls us into intimacy with Him, breaks every lie of the enemy, and frees us from condemnation and striving.

God's love is not based on what we do—it is based on who He is. His love is radical, relentless, and beyond human comprehension. It pursues us when we are lost, restores us when we return, and empowers us to live in righteousness.

I have seen firsthand how God's love transforms people. I've watched drug addicts, prisoners, and those who thought they were beyond redemption come alive in His love. And I want you to know that no matter where you've been, no matter what you've done—His love is for you.

There is always more to discover in God's love. The width, length, depth, and height of it are immeasurable. The deeper we go, the more we realize how vast His love truly is. Let this revelation become more than words on a page—let it become the very heartbeat of your life.

Call to Action

Take time today to reflect on the depth of God's love for you. Don't just settle for an intellectual knowledge of His love—seek to experience it daily. Spend time in His Word, meditate on His promises, and ask the Holy Spirit to reveal the width, depth, height, and breadth of His love.

Scriptures Referenced

- 1 John 4:9-10
- John 15:5
- 2 Corinthians 5:17
- Luke 15:11-24
- Romans 8:9-11
- Jeremiah 31:3
- John 14:9
- 1 John 3:1
- James 4:7

Chapter Three

He Is for You

There's something remarkable about walking with the Lord for years and still being undone by the depth of His love. I've known God for decades, and yet His love continues to overwhelm me. Every season, every revelation seems to unfold a deeper dimension of who He is. That's the beauty of relationship with God. His love doesn't grow old or stale; it enlarges your heart and builds your faith. And what I've come to know, time and time again, is that He is for me. He is not against me. He is not distant. He is present, intentional, and overflowing with goodness.

When we say we want to grow in our faith, we're really saying we want to know God more. And if we want to know God, then we have to study His love, because God is love (1 John 4:8). The enemy knows this, and that's why his number one strategy is to distort the true nature of God in our minds. If he can make us believe that God is angry, disappointed, or distant, then we won't draw near to Him. We'll retreat instead of pursuing. But when we understand that God is love and that He is for us, our hearts begin to heal, our faith begins to rise, and we start walking in freedom.

Knowing and Believing

It starts with knowing and believing. Not just head knowledge, but heart knowledge. First John 4:16 says, "*And we have known and believed the love that God has for us*" (*NKJV*). It's one thing to nod our heads and agree, but quite another to let that truth saturate our hearts. We need to move from a casual acknowledgment of God's love to an unwavering belief that transforms how we live. When we know and believe His love, we stop striving and start receiving.

When I talk about knowing and believing the love of God, I mean something deeper than just hearing a sermon and thinking, *Yes, that sounds right.* It's about something shifting in your heart, where you not only hear it, but you believe it for yourself. It becomes *your* identity. I remember seasons when I could quote scripture, I could sing all the right worship songs, but there was still a part of me that struggled to believe I was truly loved—no strings attached. That God didn't love me based on performance, but simply because of who He is. His love is unconditional. It doesn't fluctuate with our moods or mistakes. It remains constant, pursuing us, waiting for us to simply say yes.

There's something powerful that happens when you go from just mentally agreeing that God loves you to believing it in your core. When it becomes a belief system—not just theology—it changes how you see everything. You start interpreting your life, your struggles, and your future through the lens of love. That's when fear begins to lose its grip, because, as 1 John 4:18 says, "*Perfect love casts out fear*" (*NKJV*).

So, when challenges come, and they will, instead of saying, "Why is this happening to me?" you begin to ask, "God, how do You want to reveal Your love to me in this?" It creates a posture of expectation instead of anxiety. Believing His love means you expect His goodness. You expect His faithfulness. And you begin to experience peace that passes understanding. That's the power of knowing and believing that you are fully loved by God.

God's love is not a shallow concept. It's not just about feeling warm and fuzzy. It's about being fully convinced that He is who He says He is. That He loves you as you are and is working in every detail of your life. When you know and believe His love, fear has to go. Condemnation has to go. Shame has to go. Because you begin to see yourself the way God sees you—fully accepted and deeply cherished.

Where Surrender Leads

Another thing that happens when you trust in His love is that you begin to surrender. And I'll tell you, this is where it gets fun, because surrender isn't scary when you trust that He's good. When you know He's for you, you stop questioning and start obeying. That's the kind of surrender that leads to purpose. It moves you from passive belief to powerful trust. It's not just knowing He loves you—it's trusting Him with everything because of that love.

I remember being just ten years old when I told my teacher I wanted to be a missionary. She told me it wasn't realistic, but I knew what I felt in my heart. Later, I told her I'd be a writer instead. (Secretly, I planned to write about my missionary journeys!) That dream was planted by God. But more than a childhood calling, it became a lifestyle of surrender.

As I grew in my understanding of God's love, I came to realize that His plans were always better than mine. And the more I surrendered, the more He led me. Not just once, but daily. Every day, I lay down my planner and ask, "What do You want, Lord?" And I'll tell you—what He wants is often bigger, grander, and far more impactful than anything I could have planned.

When we surrender to God's love, we begin to experience freedom like never before. We let go of fear, striving, and self-protection. We lay down our expectations and pick up His promises. Surrendering isn't about losing—it's about gaining everything He has for us.

You Are Not the Source—He Is

When Jesus said in John 15:5, "*I am the vine; you* are *the branches*" (*NKJV*), He was setting us free. We were never meant to be the source. He is the vine. All we have to do is abide. Trying to be the source will only wear you out. I've seen moms and dads, pastors and leaders run themselves dry trying to produce fruit out of their own strength. But when you abide in Him, fruit comes naturally. Strength comes supernaturally. Peace follows effortlessly.

There have been times in my own life when I was trying to do it all. Whether it was ministry, family, or just managing the daily responsibilities, I slipped into this mindset that I had to make everything happen. That somehow, if I didn't hold it all together, everything would fall apart. But the truth is that the moment we try to be the vine, we disconnect from the very source that empowers us. I've learned, sometimes the hard way, that I wasn't created to carry it all. You weren't either.

I especially feel this is a word for parents—moms, dads, caretakers. You are not the source of your child's salvation, their healing, or their future. You can't be everything to everyone, and that is not a failure—it's freedom. You're not meant to be the answer. Jesus is. And His love, flowing through you, is more than enough.

I think about those mornings when we wake up and, instantly, our minds start racing: *What do I need to do today?* How do I fix this? What am I going to do about that situation? And in those moments, instead of turning to God first, we lean on our own understanding. We jump into the chaos, trying to manage it with our own strength. But abiding in Him means starting the day saying, "Lord, You are my source today. Fill me first."

Remaining in Him means reminding yourself, even when you're tempted to strive: "Wait—I'm the branch. I wasn't created to produce on my own. I was created to receive." And when you live that way, you're not just surviving—you're thriving. And the people around you can see it. You become someone who brings life, not because you're amazing in your own ability, but because you're connected to the One who is.

I see so many people exhausted—trying to save their families, fix their finances, and be everything to everyone. But God never asked us to be the vine. That's His job. Our role is to remain connected to Him, to draw from His love and strength. And when we do, we flourish.

Living Through Him

That's the invitation—to live through Him. "*This is how God showed his love among us: He sent his one and only Son into the world that we might live through him*" (1 John 4:9, *NIV*). Whether you're single, married, parenting, working, leading, or learning, you get to live through Him. I gave my singleness to the Lord, and it has impacted the strength of my marriage today. That love shapes how we raise our children. It has a domino effect, touching every area we surrender to Him.

I believe one of the most powerful revelations of God's love is when we stop trying to do life on our own and instead begin to live through Him. That means we stop asking God to simply bless our plans, and we begin inviting Him to be the center of them. There is such a difference when you're doing something for God versus doing it through Him. Whether it's your job, your ministry, your parenting, or your daily decisions, when you live through Him, you tap into supernatural grace, peace, and wisdom.

I've walked through seasons of ministry, marriage, motherhood, and even personal uncertainty, where the only way I made it through was by allowing the Lord to live through me. There were times when I was tired or discouraged, but I would say, "Lord, I can't do this in my own strength—but You can through me." And He always did. That's the beauty of surrendering to His love—it doesn't stop at comfort. It empowers us.

Living through Him also means you start to see every moment as an opportunity to walk in partnership with God.

From the most mundane tasks to the biggest decisions, you develop a confidence that He is right there with you. And that confidence isn't arrogance—it's rest. It's not about proving something; it's about abiding in Someone. You begin to approach your responsibilities with peace, not pressure. You stop striving and start trusting.

And here's what I love—you don't have to be in full-time ministry to live through Him. This isn't about a platform or a pulpit. This is about real life. You can live through Him in your workplace, school, business, and even your kitchen. You can invite Him into your conversations, finances, relationships, and dreams. His love doesn't just meet you in church—it meets you in the details.

Living through Him is a daily decision. It's waking up and saying, "Lord, live through me today." And as you do, your life becomes a testimony of what His love can do—not just for you, but through you.

His Banner

Song of Solomon 2:4 says, "*His banner over me was love*" (*NKJV*). In ancient Rome, banners were visual declarations of victory. They showed the enemy which cities had already been conquered. When God lifts His banner of love over your life, He's declaring to the enemy: "This one is Mine." Every area the enemy tried to defeat you in becomes a testimony of God's goodness.

I love this image because in Roman history, when their armies marched on a new city, they carried massive banners—huge flags that listed all the nations they had already conquered. These banners were carried high so that even from a distance, you could see who had already fallen. So, imagine you're standing on the wall of a city, watching the Roman army march toward you, and you begin to see the names of stronger cities than yours already defeated. It would make your heart tremble. That's exactly what the enemy experiences when he sees the love of God lifted up in your life.

When you wave the banner of God's love over your life, you're declaring that the enemy has already lost. You're reminding him of all the times God has healed you, provided for you, delivered you, and spoken life over you. And he begins to tremble because he knows he doesn't stand a chance against a believer who knows they are loved.

God's love is not just something we receive internally—it's something that marks us externally. It becomes our standard, our banner, our identity. It communicates to the world and to the enemy that we are victorious, not because of who we are, but because of whose we are. And that victory? It becomes contagious. It speaks loudly to others who are still in battle, still wondering if they are loved, if they can win, if God is real.

You may have areas in your life where the enemy has tried to bring defeat—through sickness, addiction, insecurity, or trauma. But when you let God's love reign over those areas, they become banners of His victory. You get to wave a flag that says, "God conquered this in my life. His love has won here."

Love vs. Fear

Fear is often the first sign that we need a deeper revelation of God's love. "*There is no fear in love. But perfect love drives out fear, because fear has to do with punishment. The one who fears is not made perfect in love*" (1 John 4:18, *NIV*). Whether it's fear for your future, fear over your children, fear of sickness, or fear about your identity, His love drives it out. Because His love doesn't leave room for torment. That's what fear is—torment. It robs us of peace, it robs us of rest, and it tries to take the place of God's truth.

I've talked to so many people—young and old—who are consumed with anxiety about what's ahead: their finances, their health, their relationships, their calling. I've been there too. I remember times when fear felt like this constant whisper in the back of my mind—"What if this doesn't work out? What if I'm not enough? What if I fail?" But I've learned something powerful—when fear tries to creep in, that's my signal to pause and say, "Lord, I need a revelation of Your love in this area." And every time I've asked, He has shown up with truth that silences fear.

Fear often disguises itself. It shows up as worry, stress, overthinking, people-pleasing, or even control. But at the root of all of it is a question: Can I trust God here? And the answer is found in His love. When you know He loves you perfectly, completely, and without wavering, then fear has no room to speak. His love becomes the anchor that steadies your heart.

And here's the beautiful part—His love isn't just a shield against fear. It's a weapon. It fights for your peace. It defends your identity. It silences the accuser. One of my favorite promises is found in Zephaniah 3:17: "*The Lord your God is with you, the Mighty Warrior who saves. He will take great delight in you; in his love he will no longer rebuke you, but will rejoice over you with singing*" (*NIV*). Isn't that beautiful? He's not distant. He's not angry. He's with you. He saves. He delights in you. He sings over you. That's not the voice of a harsh taskmaster—that's the voice of a loving Father.

His love quiets us. It brings peace to the places that were anxious, stability to the emotions that were swirling. I've had moments where I was so overwhelmed that the only thing I could do was sit and say, "God, I need You." And it was in those quiet moments that His love would come and settle my heart. It was as if He was saying, "I've got this. You're not alone."

If there's fear in your heart today—about your children, your future, your past, your health—ask the Lord to replace it with His perfect love. You don't need to have all the answers. You just need to know who your Father is. Because when you know He is for you, and you believe in His love, fear loses its grip. And friend, you don't have to live with fear when you're rooted in His love. That's the power of perfect love—it casts out fear and replaces it with peace, confidence, and unshakable joy.

Receiving the Fullness

So many believers stop at salvation, thinking it's just about avoiding hell. But salvation includes healing, provision, freedom, identity, authority, and joy. "*I pray that the eyes of your heart may be enlightened in order that you may know the hope to which he has called you, the riches of his glorious inheritance in his holy people*"

(Eph. 1:18, *NIV*). That inheritance is already inside of you because Christ lives in you.

And this is where the message of this chapter comes full circle—He is for you. If you ever doubt that, look at what He's made available to you through Jesus. He didn't withhold anything. His love is extravagant, and He desires that you live in the fullness of that love every single day. The cross wasn't just a ticket to heaven—it was the doorway to a life of abundance right here and now. That's the kind of God He is. That's what it means for Him to be for you.

When Jesus died, the inheritance became ours. We're not waiting until we get to heaven to enjoy it—we're called to live in it now. It's like receiving a massive inheritance and never touching it. So many believers live that way. They've heard about the promises of God, but they feel disqualified—too broken, too far gone, too unworthy. But the truth is, His love qualifies you. His grace has made a way.

I remember being on the mission field when the Lord spoke something to my heart that changed my entire perspective. He said, "Carrie, when you get to heaven, I don't want you to just hear 'Well done.' I want to look at you and say, 'You knew Me. You didn't wait until heaven—you knew Me here.'" That hit me so deeply. I realized that I wasn't called to wait until eternity to experience God's fullness. I was called to walk in it now.

When we live with the confidence that He is for us, we start receiving differently. We stop begging God for scraps and begin boldly accessing what's already been given. Healing? It's part of the inheritance. Peace? It's yours. Wisdom, joy, provision, power—all of it is evidence that you are loved and chosen by a Father who has already made up His mind about you.

And not only do you get to walk in your inheritance, but you also get to distribute it. That's how much God is for you—He wants His love to flow through you. You're not just a recipient; you're a vessel. You lay hands on the sick and see them recover. You speak words of life. You walk in abundance and bless others. That's the power of walking in your inheritance. And that's the proof that He is, and always will be, for you.

Revelation Brings Transformation

All it takes is one revelation to change everything. I've seen it time and time again. A person hears one message, and suddenly, the eyes of their heart are opened. That's what Paul prayed in Ephesians 1:18 —"*I pray that the eyes of your heart may be enlightened in order that you may know the hope to which he has called you, the riches of his glorious inheritance in his holy people*" (NIV). When our eyes are opened to truth, even just a glimpse of His love, it shifts everything.

Sometimes, we look at someone's life and think, "Wow, look at the transformation," and we imagine it took years of struggle, layers of religious discipline, or some dramatic encounter. But so often, it really comes down to one moment where the truth of God's love collides with the lies we've believed. Just one moment when His voice becomes louder than our doubts. That's what revelation does—it breaks through darkness with light.

I'll never forget the way I saw this unfold in my own husband. There were things he believed about the nature of God and how we accessed it. One night, he heard the message of grace, and I could see something shift. It wasn't emotionalism; it was revelation. And by the second night of hearing that same message, it was like I had a new husband. Everything changed because something clicked. The Holy Spirit knows exactly how to deliver that breakthrough, and when He does, the fruit is undeniable.

This is why I encourage people not to give up praying for others. Maybe you have someone in your life who seems far from God, and you've already laid out in your mind all the steps they must take to change. But God doesn't need your twelve-step plan—He just needs one moment to enlighten the eyes of their heart. So, instead of mapping out the path, start praying, "Lord, give them a revelation." Because that's what transformed my husband, that's what's transformed me, and that's what will transform the people you're believing for.

Revelation doesn't just correct our theology—it awakens our identity. It brings clarity where there was confusion. It brings purpose where there was wandering. It's not just about getting more information; it's about divine impartation. When God reveals something to your spirit, no one can take it from you. It becomes part of how you think, live, and believe.

So, wherever you are right now, ask the Lord, "What do You want me to see?" He knows exactly where to begin. You don't have to figure out everything at once. You just have to say yes to the light He's shining today. Because one revelation—just one—can shift everything.

Made for First-Class Living

I love using the analogy of flying. For years, we traveled internationally on tight budgets—always in economy. We'd fly redeyes, endure long layovers, and hunt for the cheapest tickets. But then, one day, we were upgraded. First to Economy Plus, then to Business Class. I remember sitting there thinking, "I don't know if I can go back." It wasn't just about comfort—it was about how different everything felt when you stopped scraping by and started receiving abundance.

That's what life in Christ is supposed to be like. Not just scraping by spiritually, emotionally, financially—but stepping into the fullness of what He's already made available. Psalm 84:11–12 says, "*For the Lord God is a sun and shield; the LORD bestows favor and honor. No good thing does He withhold from those who walk uprightly. O LORD of hosts, blessed is the one who trusts in you!*" (ESV). He's not holding back from you. If He didn't withhold His Son, why would He withhold anything else?

You were not designed for survival-mode Christianity. You were not meant to spend your life at the back of the plane spiritually, just hoping to make it to heaven. Jesus didn't go to the cross so you could live a life of lack, constantly questioning your worth or begging for scraps. He went to the cross to transfer you into abundance—into a life of healing, peace, joy, purpose, and provision. This is the first-class inheritance of a child of God.

I love what Deuteronomy 7:13 says: "*He will love you and bless you and multiply you; He will also bless the fruit of your womb and the fruit of your land, your grain and your new wine and your oil, the increase of your cattle and the offspring of your flock, in the land which He swore to your fathers to give you*" (NKJV). Even in the Old Testament, God made it clear—His heart has always been to love, bless, and multiply His people. That hasn't changed.

But here's the key: you have to believe that this kind of life is for you. Many believers have settled. They think, *Well, I got saved, and that's enough.* But they stop short of inheritance because they don't think they're worthy. They think the blessings are for someone else, someone more righteous, more disciplined, more spiritual. That is a lie from the enemy. God's love is the same for every child. The difference is that some receive it and walk in it. Others don't.

Friend, you were made for first-class living. Not because of anything you did—but because of who your Father is. He is for you, and He delights in lavishing His love on His children. It's time to stop apologizing for the goodness of God in your life. It's time to stop explaining away your blessings. Start walking boldly in them. Not just for your sake—but because when others see the goodness of God in your life, they'll say, "I want to know that God too."

You were made to reflect the abundance of His kingdom. So, stretch out your legs, rest in His provision, and enjoy the ride. You're not just invited into first class—you belong there.

Final Thoughts

Friend, you are deeply loved. Not just a little bit, not just when you behave, but abundantly and unconditionally. God wants you to walk in everything He's provided—healing, peace, joy, purpose, provision, identity, and strength. You don't have to earn it. You just have to believe it.

You were never meant to live in fear or lack. You were designed to abide in Him and experience His love every day. That love will not only transform your life, it will also overflow to those around you. You were made to distribute the inheritance.

Call to Action

I want to challenge and encourage you to take some real steps in responding to God's love. Ask the Lord to reveal any areas of your life where fear has replaced love and invite Him to speak truth into those spaces. Open up the Word—not casually, but expectantly—and receive His promises as personal and powerful for your life. Make surrender a daily rhythm: offer Him your plans, your pain, your dreams, and let His love guide you in return. Choose to believe—truly believe—that His love is for you, not just in theory but in your everyday, practical, ordinary life. Receive your inheritance boldly, knowing that healing, joy, wisdom, provision, and identity are not distant promises but present realities. And as you walk in that love, don't keep it to yourself—become a distributor of His goodness, blessing others with what you've received.

Scriptures Referenced

- 1 John 4:8-9
- 1 John 4:16
- 1 John 4:18
- John 15:5

- Song of Solomon 2:4
- Zephaniah 3:17
- Ephesians 1:18
- Deuteronomy 7:13
- Psalm 84:11–12

Chapter Four

The Fullness of God

When we talk about the love of God, we're not talking about a nice concept or a poetic sentiment. We're talking about the very nature of who He is. And when you truly begin to understand who He is, you start to realize that He doesn't do anything halfway. He doesn't just sprinkle blessings—He lavishes them. He doesn't love with limits—He loves to the fullest. That's what this chapter is all about: stepping into the fullness of God.

Having traveled all over the world—from India to Russia, Africa to China—I've seen so many different religions, cultures, and beliefs. And I can say this boldly: only in Jesus have I experienced the love of a real God. Not a god you have to appease with offerings and rituals. Not a god who changes moods based on your performance. But a God whose banner over you is love. A God who gave everything so you could live in the fullness of His heart.

Knowing the One True God

I'll never forget when I was seventeen years old, sitting in a small, dark house in India on a missions trip. There was a little shrine in the corner of the room filled with dozens of idols—each one meant to serve a different purpose: healing, provision, safety, and even dreams. I asked the woman who lived there, "What are these for?" And she explained which idol she prayed to for which problem. But when I asked her what was going on in her life right now, she pointed to the idol for healing and said, "It's not working."

I was heartbroken—but I was also filled with hope. Because I knew something she didn't: there is a living God who loves her and hears her. A God who doesn't require you to figure out what mood He's in or what offering you need to give. A God who gave His Son so you could come boldly to Him.

And I saw that transformation happen in those villages. People who had prayed to hundreds of gods finally met the One who created them. They found peace. They found joy. They found a love that doesn't fail. And when they understood who God really is, their lives began to overflow.

Unfailing Love

When the love of God becomes more than a theological concept—when it becomes a reality in your heart—something amazing happens. You begin to overflow. Love doesn't stay contained. It spills into your conversations, your relationships, and your prayers. You begin to walk in a boldness and peace that only comes from knowing how deeply loved you are.

First Corinthians 13:8 says, "*Love never fails. But whether* there are *prophecies, they will fail; whether* there are *tongues, they will cease; whether* there is *knowledge, it will vanish away*" (*NKJV*). What does that tell us? That even spiritual gifts, as powerful as they are, will one day fade. But love—that remains. It's eternal. It is the foundation for everything else.

And when you truly get a revelation of this unfailing love, it becomes your first response, not your last resort. You don't walk into situations panicking—you walk in declaring, "This is no problem for the love of God." That love has already conquered sickness, fear, and lack. It already broke the curse at the cross. It already made you righteous. And when you know that, you begin to minister out of confidence, not striving.

I remember being at one of our conferences at Charis Bible College, and a woman came up to me in the prayer line and said she had cancer. Without even thinking, I looked at her and said, "No problem." And I meant it. Not because I was dismissing her pain, but because I know who my God is. His love already provided the answer. His love never fails. And that's not just a nice Scripture—it's a reality I've seen over and over again.

I've seen this kind of overflow in the mission field too—people who used to pray to idols or live in fear, once they received the love of God, they couldn't help but share it. Healing began to flow. Joy returned. Whole families came to Jesus. Why? Because once love gets in, it doesn't stay in. It moves. It reaches. It overflows.

So, if you've ever felt stuck—like your faith is stagnant or your joy is on pause—ask yourself: Have I allowed His love to overflow in me? Have I really received it, or have I just agreed with it in theory? Because when it's real in your heart, it becomes real in your life. And the fruit of that is undeniable.

There's a truth that changed my life and my teaching, and it's found in Galatians 5:6: "*For in Christ Jesus neither circumcision nor uncircumcision avails anything, but faith working through love*" (*NKJV*). This verse hit me like a lightning bolt one day. It's not your performance, your spiritual resume, or your tradition that matters. What matters is this: your faith is activated by love.

When I got this revelation, everything in the Word became more personal. Promises stopped being verses on a page and started becoming declarations in my heart. Because when you understand how loved you are, you believe differently. You pray differently. You stand differently.

And I saw this in action when my sister was in the hospital for sixty-nine days, fighting for her life on a ventilator. The reports were bad. But our prayers weren't born out of desperation—they were rooted in love. We reminded each other every day: "She is loved of God." And when you believe that, your faith rises up and says, "Healing is already hers."

Faith becomes powerful when it flows from the revelation that God is for you. That's the difference between begging God to move and standing confidently in what He's already done.

Faith Working Through Love

As I mentioned before, a revelation of Galatians 5:6 had a profound impact on me: "*For in Christ Jesus neither circumcision nor uncircumcision avails anything, but faith working through love*" (*NKJV*).

I had taught God's love all over the world—in Russia, Congo, and India—but it wasn't until I saw this verse during a teaching with my husband that the Lord peeled back another layer. Suddenly, I realized that every promise in the Word becomes mine when I believe it through the lens of love. It's not about striving to earn it or perform for it—it's about knowing I'm already loved.

You see, when you understand God's love, your faith has something solid to stand on. You read the Word differently. "By His stripes I am healed"—that's not wishful thinking anymore. That's truth rooted in love. You stop begging and start declaring: "This is mine because God loves me."

During my sister's battle with COVID, this became more than theory. Day after day, as she lay in a hospital bed, sedated and ventilated, we stood on the Word—not in desperation, but in love-fueled faith. We said, "She is loved of God, so healing is hers." And I watched a miracle unfold—not because we were perfect, but because we believed in a perfect love.

This is how faith works when it's flowing from love: it isn't afraid to speak boldly. It doesn't collapse when the report is bad. It stands up and says, "No, this situation must bow to the love of God."

When your faith is working through love, you're no longer trying to convince God to move—you're standing on what He already accomplished. That's the kind of faith that moves mountains. That's the kind of faith that makes the devil nervous when you wake up in the morning.

So, if your faith has felt weak or your prayers have seemed powerless, ask the Lord to renew your revelation of His love. Because when you're rooted in love, your faith won't waver. It won't question if God hears. It will know: I'm loved, and His promises are mine.

The Power of Abiding

In John 15:8–10, Jesus says, "*By this My Father is glorified, that you bear much fruit; so you will be My disciples. As the Father loved Me, I also have loved you; abide in My love. If you keep My commandments, you will abide in My love, just as I have kept My Father's commandments and abide in His love*" (NKJV).

Abiding in God's love is not a one-time decision; it's a daily invitation to remain in Him. Jesus is calling us to a lifestyle of staying in His love—not just visiting it during church or devotions, but letting it be the atmosphere of our entire lives.

When I read this verse, I'm reminded that the Father loved Jesus with such perfect, eternal love—and that same love is extended to us. That's breathtaking. Jesus is saying, "I've loved you with the same love the Father loved Me. Now, stay in it. Abide in it."

We don't abide through obligation; we abide through revelation. The more we understand who God is and how He sees us, the more we *want* to stay close to Him. And abiding always leads to fruit. The Father is glorified when our lives bear much fruit—not by our own efforts, but because we're connected to the source.

This Word becomes the vine that connects us. Jesus said that if we keep His commandments, we will abide in His love. That doesn't mean we earn His love—it means we respond to it. Keeping His Word is not about legalism; it's about love. We obey because we trust. We follow because we're loved.

And when we stay in that abiding place, we stop striving to produce results. We simply rest in Him, and fruit begins to grow. Peace in chaos. Joy in trials. Strength in weakness. Wisdom in confusion. All of it flows from staying connected to the One who is love.

That's the power of abiding: it's not about how strong you are—it's about how deeply rooted you are in the One who never changes, never fails, and always loves.

Transformed by Truth

There is something so powerful that happens when your mind is renewed by truth. Romans 12:2 says, "*Do not be conformed to this world, but be transformed by the renewing of your mind, that you may prove what* is *that good and acceptable and perfect will of God*" (*NKJV*). This isn't just about memorizing verses or attending Bible studies. It's about letting the truth of who God is reshape how you see everything—yourself, your circumstances, your future.

When you're transformed by truth, you stop filtering your identity through your past or your failures. You begin to see yourself through the lens of who He says you are. You start to think, *Wait a minute, I'm not just trying to survive—I'm more than a conqueror. I'm not a victim—I'm victorious because of Christ in me.*

That transformation doesn't happen by accident. It comes from time spent in the Word, letting it mirror back to you who you really are. Like I tell our students at Charis Bible College, this Word is not just information—it's revelation. It's the Spirit of God showing you who He is, and in turn, who you are in Him.

And I've seen it happen in real time. I've seen people who came into our classrooms bound by shame, addiction, and fear—and as the Word got in them, something broke loose. Their posture changed. Their speech changed. Their faith ignited. Why? Because they were being transformed by truth.

This isn't about striving for change. This is about surrendering to the love and truth of a God who already sees you as whole. And when that truth becomes more real than your feelings or your past, transformation is inevitable.

So, let the Word work. Let it do what only it can do. And don't be surprised when the old thoughts no longer stick, and the lies no longer hold weight. Because truth—God's truth—liberates you from the inside out.

Living in the Overflow

When you know who God is, you begin to recognize what He's already placed inside of you. And that changes everything. You stop waiting for something external to happen and start living from the abundance already within.

Ephesians 3:19 says, "*To know the love of Christ which passes knowledge; that you may be filled with all the fullness of God*" (*NKJV*). That means this isn't just about head knowledge—it's about being so rooted in His love that you carry the fullness of God everywhere you go. You become a vessel of His presence, a carrier of His heart.

Overflow isn't just about receiving; it's about releasing. You realize, "I've been given so much, how can I not give it away?" Your life becomes a testimony of who God is—not because everything's perfect, but because you're anchored in a perfect love.

I remember times when I didn't feel like I had anything to give. Moments when I was weary, stretched thin, unsure. But I've learned that when I go back to the source—when I abide in His love—the overflow returns. It's not about mustering strength. It's about staying connected.

The overflow of God's love touches every area of your life: your family, your work, your decisions, your emotions. It becomes the filter through which you see the world. You stop reacting to pressure and start responding from peace. You stop striving for approval and start living from acceptance.

This is what it means to live in the fullness of God: not just to receive His love, but to be so full of it that it spills out onto everyone around you. And that kind of life? It's irresistible. It's contagious. It's the gospel in motion.

Knowing You're Anointed

One of the most freeing revelations I've ever had in my walk with God is this: I don't need a title or a platform to be anointed.

I just need Jesus. First John 2:20 says, "*But you have an anointing from the Holy One, and you know all things*" (*NKJV*). Isn't that powerful? That means you don't have to wait to be approved by people or recognized by the world. You've already been chosen. You've already been filled.

You see, the enemy loves to whisper, "Who do you think you are?" He wants to point to your past, your failures, your insecurities. But when you know you're anointed, you can look at him and say, "I know exactly who I am. I'm a child of God, filled with His Spirit, and walking in His authority."

I remember being on the mission field, and there were moments when I felt completely out of my depth. I wasn't the most experienced. I didn't have all the answers. But I had the Holy Spirit. And that's all I needed. As I stepped out in faith—whether preaching, praying, or ministering to one person in a small village—I knew I was walking in an anointing that didn't come from me. It came from Him.

And here's the beautiful connection to the fullness of God: when you recognize that you've been anointed by God, you stop striving to become something and start living from what already is. The fullness of God isn't something you earn—it's something you carry. And that anointing equips you to love the unlovable, speak truth with grace, heal the sick, and bring light into darkness.

So, if you've ever felt unqualified—welcome to the club. But also know this: your qualification doesn't come from man. It comes from your Creator. And He says you are chosen, called, anointed, and equipped. When you walk in that identity, the fullness of God flows through you.

The world doesn't need more perfect people. It needs anointed believers who know who they are and Who lives in them. You are anointed to bring the kingdom wherever you go—and that's not a maybe. That's a promise.

Final Thoughts

We've covered so much in this chapter, but it all comes back to one truth: God is for you. And if He is for you, who can be against you? He didn't save you so you could barely survive—He saved you so you could live in the fullness of His love and victory.

This love changes how we see ourselves, how we walk through trials, how we pray, and how we relate to the world. It transforms us from the inside out. You don't have to wait for heaven to know God deeply. He wants you to know Him now. To abide in Him now. To walk in fullness now.

There is no shortage in heaven. God's not rationing out His blessings. His love is vast, deep, wide, and high. And He wants you to experience it daily. He wants you to overflow.

Call to Action

Take time this week to sit with the Lord and ask Him to show you areas of your life where He wants to pour out more of His fullness. Open the Word and declare His promises—not as distant hopes, but as present realities secured by His love. Ask the Holy Spirit to reveal any lies you've believed about your identity, worth, or qualification. Replace them with truth. And don't just receive this love for yourself—let it overflow. Pray for someone. Speak a word of encouragement. Lay hands on the sick. Live like someone who knows they are loved and filled with the fullness of God.

Scriptures Referenced

- Galatians 5:6
- 1 Corinthians 13:8
- Ephesians 3:19
- John 15:8–10
- Romans 12:2
- 1 John 2:20

Chapter Five

How He Sees You

Every time I minister on God's love, it ministers right back to me. That's the power of love—real, divine love. When we talk about God's love, we are getting straight to the heart of the Father and the very core of the Gospel. This love story, the Bible, from Genesis to Revelation, is about His love moving toward us. If you've journeyed through the previous chapters, you know we've already laid a powerful foundation. But in this chapter, we're going deeper—into how love not only saves us but transforms our very identity. This is about seeing ourselves the way He sees us.

God's love is more than an emotion or a theological concept; it is the driving force behind your faith, your confidence, and your authority as a believer. Let this be a time of receiving—not just information, but revelation. The kind of revelation that sets you free from fear, shame, and the lies of the enemy. This chapter is a declaration: You are who God says you are because you are deeply, consistently, and eternally loved. And how He sees you is what defines you.

Love Casts Out Fear and Ignites Faith

There is no fear in love. That's what the Word of God says in 1 John 4:18:

> *There is no fear in love. But perfect love drives out fear, because fear has to do with punishment. The one who fears is not made perfect in love (NIV).*

Fear and love cannot coexist. When God's love is perfected in you, fear is evicted. His love becomes the environment in which faith grows.

In Galatians 5:6, we read:

> *For in Christ Jesus neither circumcision nor uncircumcision has any value. The only thing that counts is faith expressing itself through love (NIV).*

That means faith isn't rooted in works, appearance, or outward qualifications. Faith finds its power source in love. When you are convinced that you are loved, you can believe for anything. When you know you're cherished by God, you step into faith, not with striving, but with trust.

I shared previously that my sister was on a ventilator during the COVID crisis. I could have allowed fear to take over. Everything in the natural was shouting panic. But something rose up in us because we had a revelation of God's love. That love gave us confidence to stand in faith, to speak life, to pray boldly—not from desperation, but from a place of trust. Faith came alive because love had been rooted deep within us.

See, when you know how much you are loved, your prayers change. Your attitude shifts. The Word starts reading you, not the other way around. It becomes personal. It becomes alive.

"Because He loved me, He gave me this. Because I'm loved, I'm redeemed from that."

You begin to see every verse, every promise, not as a distant hope, but a present inheritance. And that's the shift—when you read the Word, not through the lens of condemnation, but through the lens of love.

We're not checking boxes to earn approval. We're standing on promises because we know we're already loved. Faith then becomes natural, even bold. Because the God who gave us these promises is love, and He never lies.

So, I want to ask you: what fear is trying to rule you? What lie is trying to keep you small? Let God's love drive that fear out today. Not by your effort, but by letting His love go deeper than it ever has before.

Written in Love

To truly understand how God sees you, you must understand how He speaks to you—and that begins with the Word. The Bible isn't a rulebook written to condemn you. It is a love letter written by a Father who wants you to know Him, walk with Him, and see yourself the way He sees you.

First John 4:8 says,

Whoever does not love does not know God, because God is love (NIV).

That's a powerful truth. God doesn't just feel love. He *is* love. And because He is love, everything He has said and done flows from that identity. When He inspired the Scriptures, He breathed His love into every page. That means the entire Word of God—from Genesis to Revelation—was written through the lens of love.

But here's the challenge: if we approach the Word while condemning ourselves, we will read it through the wrong lens.

If we are condemning ourselves all the time—"I'm never good enough"—and read the Word with that opinion, the devil is right there to say, "See? You failed again."

I remember in my early years on the mission field in Russia, struggling with my own sense of inadequacy. I would open my Bible and sometimes feel overwhelmed—not by conviction, but by condemnation. I felt I wasn't measuring up. But then the Lord spoke to me clearly. He said, "You're reading this as if I'm trying to show you what you're not. But I'm trying to show you who you are." That was a turning point. I began to read the Word differently.

I started marking every place I saw God's love. I put red hearts in the margins of my Bible, and soon my pages were filled with them. It became a living testimony that this Word—this book we hold in our hands—isn't just a record of commands. It's a revelation of how He sees us.

When you remain in the Word—not out of duty, but from a place of relationship—you begin to experience a completion.

The love of God is perfected in you, and the Word becomes more than ink on paper. It becomes a mirror reflecting how God sees you.

When you see yourself through the Word, through His love, your identity begins to align with heaven's perspective. You begin to say, "That's who I am. That's how He sees me." And suddenly, the Bible is no longer just a spiritual discipline—it's a daily encounter with your Father's love.

Your Identity Begins with Being a Child of God

If you want to know how God sees you, start here: He sees you as His child. Not a servant groveling for approval. Not a stranger trying to prove your worth. You are His beloved, born from His will, chosen by His grace.

John 1:12–13 says,

> *But as many as received Him, to them He gave the right to become children of God, to those who believe in His name: who were born, not of blood, nor of the will of the flesh, nor of the will of man, but of God (NKJV).*

You were not an accident. You were not merely the product of human desire or circumstance. You were born of God. And that means your identity is rooted in something eternal. When you believed in Jesus, He didn't just save you from something—He brought you *into* something. Into a family. Into a name. Into sonship.

Galatians 3:26 reaffirms it:

> *For you are all sons of God through faith in Christ Jesus (NKJV).*

This isn't about gender. This is about position. About status. Sons and daughters of God with full access and full inheritance.

I'll never forget how this became real to me. My mom had me very young, and during her senior year of high school, I stayed with my great-grandmother during the day. And let me tell you—I was her favorite. I would get to circle whatever I wanted in the J.C. Penney catalog, and she would get it for me. Not once a year. Multiple times! Why? Because I was loved. I never questioned it.

And because I knew I was loved, I walked in a boldness around her. I approached her with confidence because I knew she delighted in me.

That's how our Father sees us. He has made it abundantly clear in His Word and by His Spirit that you are His favorite. He has given you the right to come boldly. When you believe in the name of Jesus, you become part of the family—not on probation but fully embraced.

And here's where the lies of the enemy fall apart: it doesn't matter where you come from. It doesn't matter about your past. It doesn't matter what's been said about you. Because how God sees you overrides every other voice.

You don't have to live by your earthly lineage anymore. You don't have to replay the voice of Aunt so-and-so or the failures of your upbringing. You've been born of God. You are in the household of faith now. And that comes with all the blessings, all the promises, and all the love of a perfect Father.

You get a revelation of God's love for you, and Aunt so-and-so's opinion doesn't have the power to tell you what your identity is.

It's time to see yourself as He sees you: a cherished child. A welcome son or daughter. A full member of the royal family. That's not just something to believe for—it's who you are. Right now.

You Are a Son with Full Rights

Salvation doesn't make you a second-class citizen in the kingdom—it makes you a son or daughter with full rights. And yet, so many believers live like spiritual beggars. They think, *Well, I'm saved, and that's more than I deserve, so I won't expect anything more.* But when you truly understand how He sees you—as a fully adopted child—the way you see yourself can be completely transformed.

Galatians 4:4–7 lays it out so beautifully:

> *But when the set time had fully come, God sent his Son, born of a woman, born under the law, to redeem those under the law, that we might receive adoption to sonship. Because you are his sons, God sent the Spirit of his Son into our hearts, the Spirit who calls out, 'Abba, Father.' So you are no longer a slave, but God's child; and since you are his child, God has made you also an heir* (NIV).

This isn't symbolic language—this is the real deal. You are not a slave, fearing rejection and trying to earn your place. You are His child. You've been adopted, and with that adoption comes every right, every promise, and every blessing.

I remember early in my ministry days, I was surrounded by others who seemed to walk in more confidence and authority. I admired them, but I also compared myself. I would think, *Maybe they're more anointed. Maybe they're just more favored.* But God began to speak something deep into my spirit: "Carrie, you are My daughter with full rights. There's no 'less-than' in the kingdom."

Many believers walk around thinking that others are more loved, more chosen. But God doesn't play favorites. What He has given to one child, He offers to all. That includes you.

I love the picture of the throne room from Hebrews 4:16:

> *Let us therefore come boldly to the throne of grace, that we may obtain mercy and find grace to help in time of need (NKJV).*

When you know how He sees you, you don't tiptoe into His presence. You don't wait until you've got it all together. You *run*—boldly, confidently. You jump right up on the lap of the King of kings and say, "Dad, here's what's going on." And He listens. Not because of what you've done, but because of who you are: His child.

I once got a picture in prayer of a royal throne room. Golden pillars, angelic hosts, immense splendor—and then a little barefoot kid running full speed through the doors, giggling, hair a mess, just bursting through security straight to the throne. The guards didn't stop him. You know why? Because that was the king's son. That kind of access wasn't earned—it was inherited.

You have that kind of access.

You don't have to beg God to hear you. You don't have to earn His love. You have full rights, full inheritance, and full status as His child. That means healing, provision, joy, peace, purpose—all of it belongs to you.

So, how does He see you? He sees you as a son. He sees you as a daughter. Not one barely making it in, but fully embraced and fully empowered.

You're not just in the family. You carry the family name. You walk in the family's authority. And heaven backs you because your Father is the King.

You Are Cleansed

One of the greatest lies the enemy whispers is that your past still defines you—that the mistakes you made, the regrets you carry, and the things you're ashamed of somehow disqualify you. But God doesn't see you through the lens of your sin. He sees you through the finished work of the cross. He sees you as pure.

First John 1:9 tells us this:

> *If we confess our sins, He is faithful and just to forgive us* our *sins and to cleanse us from all unrighteousness* (*NKJV*).

Not *some* unrighteousness. Not just the easy stuff. Not only what happened before you got saved. **All** unrighteousness. That means every mistake, every failure, every wound you've carried—washed clean.

The word "cleanse" here doesn't just mean covered. It means completely removed. It's not God saying, "Okay, I'll forgive it, but I'm still watching you." No, He says, "I don't see it anymore." You are as clean as Jesus because Jesus became sin *for you.*

Second Corinthians 5:21 says it like this:

> *For He made Him who knew no sin* to be *sin for us, that we might become the righteousness of God in Him* (NKJV).

That is how He sees you—righteous. Not because of your performance, but because of His sacrifice. When Jesus took your sin, He gave you His righteousness in return. That's the great exchange. And now, when the Father looks at you, He sees you through the perfection of His Son.

I remember sharing the story of the prodigal son in a previous message, and it's one of my favorites. The son came home rehearsing his repentance speech—thinking he'd have to earn his way back into the household. But before he could even get the words out, the father ran to him, embraced him, and immediately called for the best robe.

That robe wasn't just about honor. It represented righteousness. It covered his filth, his shame, and his wandering. And that's what God did for you and me. But it was more than just a covering—it was a cleansing. When we came home, He washed us clean *and* clothed us in His righteousness. The old is gone. The new has come.

Romans 3:23 reminds us:

> *For all have sinned and fall short of the glory of God* (NKJV).

That includes everyone. But the story doesn't end there. Romans 3:24 continues:

> *And all are justified freely by his grace through the redemption that came by Christ Jesus* (*NIV*).

To be justified means to be declared "not guilty." It's as if you had never sinned. That's how He sees you.

And I know—some days you don't *feel* righteous. Some days, the enemy tries to drag up the past or throw shame at you like a heavy blanket. But you need to talk back. You need to say, "No, I've been made pure. I've been cleansed. That's not who I am anymore."

This is more than a concept—it's an identity. You're not an unrighteous sinner trying to be holy. You're a righteous son or daughter learning to live from the purity you already possess in Christ.

I love what it says in 2 Corinthians 5:17:

> *Therefore, if anyone* is *in Christ,* he is *a new creation; old things have passed away; behold, all things have become new* (*NKJV*).

Not *some* things. **All things**.

So, let me ask you: Are you still defining yourself by your worst moment? Or will you begin to agree with how He sees you?

He sees you as cleansed. He sees you as new. He sees you as righteous. He sees you as pure. And His opinion is the only one that counts.

Made Complete

If you've ever felt like a broken piece trying to fit into God's big picture, you are not alone. But I want to encourage you with this: God's love doesn't just patch us up—it makes us complete. Whole. Lacking nothing. That's how He sees you.

Let's look at Colossians 2:9–10:

For in Christ all the fullness of the Deity lives in bodily form, and in Christ you have been brought to fullness. He is the head over every power and authority (NIV).

In Jesus, all the fullness of God resides. And because you are in Christ, that fullness now dwells in you. You have been made complete—not by your achievements, not by time healing wounds, but by the indwelling presence of Jesus.

I remember when I was in Russia, deep in the mission field, asking the Lord to show me how to grow in His love. I was surrounded by deep brokenness—orphans, the elderly, the addicted, and the abused. And yet in the midst of that, the Lord whispered, "Let Me love them through you, and let Me show you how much I love you." I began to see the Word differently. I saw that God's love wasn't just a soft encouragement—it was a transforming power that could make people whole, no matter how broken their past.

You may feel like parts of your heart or history are too far gone. But there's nothing His love cannot reach. He restores what the enemy tried to devour.

Joel 2:25 says,

I will restore to you the years that the swarming locust has eaten... (ESV).

That means even the things that seem lost forever—God can bring them back with abundance.

First John 2:5 says,

But if anyone obeys his word, love for God is truly made complete in them. This is how we know we are in him (NIV).

As we abide in the Word and allow the love of God to rewrite how we see ourselves, we begin to walk in a wholeness that isn't just emotional—it's spiritual. We see through a different lens. Not one of wounds, but of wonder.

And here's something powerful: when you let God's love touch every area, it transforms every area. Your identity, your relationships, your confidence, your healing—it all begins to shift. Not because you're trying harder, but because you're agreeing with how He sees you.

The love of God can transform anything you let it touch.

And that includes you.

As He Is, So Are You

One of the most transformative revelations in Scripture is found in 1 John 4:17:

> *Love has been perfected among us in this: that we may have boldness in the day of judgment; because as He is, so are we in this world* (NKJV).

This verse doesn't just speak to our eternity; it speaks to our identity now. It's not saying, "As He is, so we will be one day in heaven." It says, "*so are we in this world.*" Right now. That's how He sees you. And when you begin to see yourself that way, you now have a supernatural perspective.

When I was a student at Charis Bible College, Andrew Wommack taught on this passage, and I remember thinking, *Wait—what? As Jesus is, so am I now?* I mean, I wanted to be like Him, but this verse said I already was—in my spirit. That truth shook me. I started declaring it over myself. I would say, "As He is—victorious, pure, anointed, wise—so am I in this world."

Let me tell you—that kind of truth will push back every lie the enemy tries to throw your way.

This doesn't mean we're perfect in the natural. We still have areas of growth. But in our born-again spirit, we are already one with Him. We aren't waiting to be qualified—He already made us qualified. That's how God sees you. Not someday. Now.

Romans 8:11 affirms this incredible truth:

> *But if the Spirit of Him who raised Jesus from the dead dwells in you, He who raised Christ from the dead will also give life to your mortal bodies through His Spirit who dwells in you* (NKJV).

That same Spirit lives in you—not a watered-down version, not a baby Jesus, not just potential for holiness. The fullness of God dwells in you because you are in Christ, and Christ is in you.

I remember growing up in a small ranching town with about 350 people. I was homeschooled and didn't have the world's credentials. No degree, no formal theology training—just a calling. And when the Lord called me to Russia, to missions, to ministering and teaching, I thought, *Who am I to do this?* But then I remembered 1 John 4:17: "As He is, so am I." That became my foundation.

You don't need to apologize for who you are in Christ. You don't need to disqualify yourself because of your past, or your personality, or your shortcomings. Because when God looks at you, He sees Jesus.

As He is—righteous, full of peace, powerful, holy, and beloved—so are you in this world.

So, when the enemy whispers, "You're not good enough, or You're not spiritual enough, or You can't make a difference," you can answer confidently, "Actually, I am as He is. That's how God sees me. And that's how I choose to see myself too."

This is not arrogance. This is boldness grounded in love. God's perfect love gives us boldness—yes, even in the day of judgment. But also in every single day we live right now.

How He sees you is how you get to live.

You Are Victorious

One of the most empowering revelations of how God sees you is this: He sees you as victorious. You are not trying to earn victory—you are living from it. That's your position as His child.

First John 5:4–5 makes it clear:

> *For whatever is born of God overcomes the world. And this is the victory that has overcome the world—our faith. Who is he who overcomes the world, but he who believes that Jesus is the Son of God?* (*NKJV*).

God doesn't see you as a victim of this world's systems. He doesn't see you as someone barely making it. He sees you as an overcomer—strong, equipped, and full of faith. That's your identity in Christ.

I remember a season when the pressures of ministry, finances, and transitions hit us all at once. It felt like every area of life was under attack. But I heard the Lord speak so clearly: "Carrie, you're not under this. You're over this. Because you're born of Me." And in that moment, I was reminded—my position is not beneath. It's seated with Him in heavenly places (Eph. 2:6).

The world may bring pressure, but you have a faith that is not of this world. And that faith is activated by love. Remember Galatians 5:6 says:

> *The only thing that counts is faith expressing itself through love* (*NIV*).

That means when you know how deeply you're loved, you don't shrink back in adversity. You rise up. You declare, "This may be happening around me, but it will not define me. I overcome by faith."

Inflation, disease, dysfunction, rejection—none of it gets the final word. Faith does. And faith works by love.

You're not small. You're not powerless. You are filled with the Spirit of the Living God, and you carry the victory of Jesus inside you. That's how He sees you—not struggling but overcoming.

So, what does an overcomer look like? Someone who faces challenges head-on, not because they have all the answers, but because they know Who lives inside them. Someone who declares the Word in the face of opposition. Someone who stands firm when the enemy tries to intimidate. Someone who refuses to let their story end in defeat.

And that someone is you.

Let this truth settle deep in your heart: You overcome not because you are strong in yourself, but because you are born of God. That is your source of victory.

That is how He sees you.

Final Thoughts

When you begin to see yourself the way He sees you, through the power of God's love, it becomes the lens through which you interpret your entire life. Suddenly, your past no longer holds shame. Your present is no longer ruled by fear. And your future is no longer defined by uncertainty.

When you know how deeply you are loved by God, you stop striving to become something and start living from the truth that you already are someone. Someone chosen. Someone redeemed. Someone righteous. That's the difference between a life of performance and a life of promise.

You are not what the world says you are. You are not what your emotions scream. You are who God says you are, and His voice always echoes love. This love does more than soothe—it shapes. It transforms. It completes.

He doesn't just tolerate you. He delights in you.

And as we've walked through this chapter—verse by verse, truth by truth—we've uncovered a picture of how He sees you: fearless, full of faith, a cherished child, a rightful heir, made righteous, made whole, a reflection of Jesus Himself, and an overcomer in every circumstance.

Every story was known by Jesus on the cross. Every story was finished there. And His love starts a new chapter.

That includes your story. No matter what has marked your past, His love now defines your future. So, let the Word renew your mind. Let His Spirit remind you. Let His love reveal the truth: You are who He says you are. You are loved. You are chosen. You are righteous. You are whole. You are His.

Call to Action

Take time this week to:

- Declare Your Identity—Speak out loud the truths about who you are.
- Invite His Love—Let His love touch areas you've kept hidden or broken.
- Meditate on the Word—Mark every verse about God's love. Let it be planted in your heart.
- Stand in Boldness—Run boldly into God's throne room. You belong there.

Don't let this chapter be just a teaching. Let it be a transformation.

Scriptures Referenced

- 1 John 4:8
- 1 John 2:5
- 1 John 4:18
- Hebrews 4:16
- Galatians 5:6
- John 1:12-13
- Joel 2:25
- Galatians 3:26
- Galatians 4:4-7
- 1 John 1:9
- 2 Corinthians 5:21
- Colossians 2:9-10
- 2 Corinthians 5:17
- Romans 8:11
- Romans 3:23
- Ephesians 2:6
- 1 John 4:17
- 1 John 5:4-5

Chapter Six

Fearless Identity

Notice this book isn't titled *Your Love for God*. That's not the focus, and for good reason. This message isn't about how well we pray, read, serve, or crucify our flesh. While those things are good and have value, they can never be the foundation of our lives. If all we do comes from our effort to love God, it will always be limited. But when we begin to understand how deeply *He* loves *us*, we come to a whole new place of living. The Word says, "*We love Him because He first loved us*" (1 John 4:19, *NKJV*). That's our starting point. God's love is the fuel that empowers a fearless identity. Only by knowing that we are loved completely, unconditionally, and eternally can we step into the boldness of who we truly are in Christ.

God's Love as the Foundation

Many people live under the assumption that God is disappointed in them. They think God is looking at their failures and shortcomings, tallying up their mistakes. But that's not how He sees us. When God looks at you, He says, "You are My child. I love you. I have good things for you." This is why understanding

God's love is the starting point for everything else. It's the very foundation of our identity, behavior, and purpose.

The enemy wants to convince us that God's approval is performance-based. He whispers, "You haven't done enough. You should be praying more. You're not as spiritual as others." But God is not evaluating you based on your ability to strive. He's inviting you to rest in His love. It's only when we are rooted in that love that true transformation begins.

You may ask, "Does this mean we don't need to love or serve God?" Of course not. But true service, true love for others, and a heart that reflects Christ only come when we realize we're not doing it to earn love. We serve because we know we *are* loved. And that love produces a domino effect—your heart changes, your relationships shift, your perspective transforms.

As Scripture reminds us:

We love Him because He first loved us.

1 John 4:19, *NKJV*

Fearless Identity in Christ

God's love doesn't just make us feel good; it redefines who we are. When you grasp His love, your identity becomes rooted in truth. You realize you're not some broken, barely saved Christian limping through life. You are whole. You are His.

When you truly believe you are loved, you stop looking for validation elsewhere. You're not living to gain approval from people, your past, or your own standards. You start living from approval—God's approval. His Word becomes the mirror you look into, and what you see reflected is His righteousness in you.

We've spent time in this book talking about the revelation of identity: that you are a child of God, that you have full rights, and that you are pure and free from unrighteousness. You're not "kind of saved." You've been made complete in Him. And not only are you complete—you are victorious.

> *Love has been perfected among us in this: that we may have boldness in the day of judgment; because as He is, so are we in this world.*
>
> 1 John 4:17, *NKJV*

> *For whom He foreknew, He also predestined to be conformed to the image of His Son ... Moreover whom He predestined, these He also called; whom He called, these He also justified; and whom He justified, these He also glorified.*
>
> Romans 8:29-30, *NKJV*

> *For we are His workmanship, created in Christ Jesus for good works, which God prepared beforehand that we should walk in them.*
>
> Ephesians 2:10, *NKJV*

You're not barely making it. You're an overcomer, filled with the Spirit, walking in the fullness of God now—not someday in heaven. Right now, you reflect the image of Christ in this world. That is fearless identity.

The Great Exchange Through Grace

One of the most powerful revelations about God's love is the great exchange that happened at the cross. Jesus took on our sin, our shame, our poverty—and in exchange, He gave us righteousness, peace, abundance, and joy.

This isn't just an idea—it's a transaction. He gave up everything so we could gain everything. That's love. That's grace.

> *For you know the grace of our Lord Jesus Christ, that though He was rich, yet for your sakes He became poor, that you through His poverty might become rich.*
>
> 2 Corinthians 8:9, *NKJV*

We often reduce this to spiritual richness only. But Paul is talking about a tangible inheritance that impacts your earthly life. His love affects your provision, your peace, and your ability to walk through life with assurance.

Grace is where God says, "You couldn't do it—I'll do it for you." It's where He says, "Let me carry your pain, your sin, your sickness. Let me give you beauty for ashes, the oil of gladness for mourning." It's not based on merit. It's not based on your behavior. It's based on the goodness and love of God.

This great exchange also reveals that nothing is withheld from you. You have access to the fullness of the kingdom now. And when you believe this, you live boldly, knowing that your life is saturated with promise and provision.

Beloved Identity

When you begin to understand your identity in Christ, you realize that one of the first things God calls you is *beloved*. That's not just a poetic phrase—it's a name. It's your title in heaven.

> *I* am *my beloved's, and my beloved* is *mine. He feeds* his flock *among the lilies.*
>
> Song of Solomon 6:3, *NKJV*

God is not ashamed of you. He's not distant. He delights in you. When He looks at you, He doesn't see a failure. He sees His beloved.

My husband, after twenty-two years of being a believer, finally encountered grace. Until then, every time he opened the Bible, he felt God was calling him names: failure, disappointment, sinner. But it wasn't God's voice—it was the enemy's condemnation. Once he received a revelation of grace, the names changed: Beloved. Son. Child of Mine.

Some of us have internalized names that are not from God—rejected, unqualified, insignificant. But beloved, God is calling you to something different. He's not using your past to define your future. He's speaking over you the truth of who you really are.

You may not feel beloved, but this truth is not rooted in feeling. It's rooted in God's unchanging love. His declaration over your life stands, even when your emotions waver. Identity is not about what you feel. It's about what He said.

Victory Through Love

Understanding the love of God transforms how we respond to hardship and spiritual warfare. When we truly know we are loved, it produces an unshakeable confidence in the midst of chaos. We begin to see challenges through the lens of victory rather than defeat.

There's a lie that's crept into much of the Church—that God sends trouble to teach us a lesson. But we need to be clear: God does not do evil. He does not use the weapons of the enemy to shape His children. Cancer, loss, rejection—those are not God's tools. They are the enemy's attempts to derail and destroy. Yet in God's love, even what the enemy intends for harm, God redeems and works for our good.

> *And we know that all things work together for good to those who love God, to those who are the called according to* His *purpose*
>
> Romans 8:28, *NKJV*

When we face trials, we can respond not with fear but with assurance. Because we are loved, we can rise up in faith. God is not against you—He is always for you. Paul goes on to write:

> *What then shall we say to these things? If God is for us, who can be against us?*
>
> Romans 8:31, *NKJV*

These aren't just nice words. They are the voice of someone who knows that love gives us victory. Love gives us boldness to speak back to the enemy. When the devil tells you that you're going under, you can say, "No, I am the beloved of God. I will overcome."

And when you speak with that kind of conviction—fueled by love—it changes everything. That's the fearless identity that refuses to cower or compromise.

Freedom from Fear and the Love of Man

There is no fear in love. Yet so many of us live captive to it—fear of rejection, fear of failure, fear of what others think. The root of much of our anxiety is the belief that we are not enough, or that we have to measure up to others' standards.

> *There is no fear in love; but perfect love casts out fear, because fear involves torment. But he who fears has not been made perfect in love*
>
> 1 John 4:18, *NKJV*

In my experience, sometimes the loudest condemning voice isn't even the devil—it's our own. The enemy just stirs the pot and then lets us do the talking. "I'm not good enough. I'm not smart enough. I'll never be like them."

But the love of God comes in and rewrites the script. You no longer live under the fear of man. You no longer need their applause to feel seen. You no longer need the comparison trap to define your worth. When you receive the perfect love of God, fear loses its grip.

And this freedom isn't arrogance. It's not defiance. It's peace. It's the calm, rooted assurance that comes from knowing who you belong to. You begin to serve and love others—not because you need something from them, but because you already have everything in Christ.

Divine Workmanship and Purpose

God didn't just save you *from* something—He saved you *for* something. You are His workmanship. You are not an accident. You are not just trying to survive. You are created with divine intention.

> *For we are His workmanship, created in Christ Jesus for good works, which God prepared beforehand that we should walk in them.*
>
> Ephesians 2:10, *NKJV*

The enemy will always try to attack your image—what you look like, how much you make, how successful you are. But the love of God breaks that hold. You no longer have to live under the pressure of appearances. Your worth is not based on your weight, your wardrobe, your resume, or your relationship status.

The foundation of your purpose is not your performance. It is grace. Paul writes:

> *For by grace you have been saved through faith, and that not of yourselves;* it is *the gift of God, not of works, lest anyone should boast*
>
> Ephesians 2:8-9, *NKJV*

You don't have to hustle to earn your worth. You don't have to build a platform to prove you're valuable. You are God's workmanship—His design, His idea, His creation.

David echoed this in the Psalms:

> *For You formed my inward parts; You covered me in my mother's womb. I will praise You, for I am fearfully* and *wonderfully made; Marvelous are Your works, and* that *my soul knows very well.*
>
> Psalm 139:13-14, *NKJV*

You were made in secret, with love, with intention. Every part of your life was known and written by God. You are fearfully set apart. You don't have to conform to the world's mold.

> *Do not be conformed to this world, but be transformed by the renewing of your mind...*
>
> Romans 12:2, *NKJV*

When you let God define you, you begin to walk in purpose, with clarity and confidence. You begin to speak differently. You carry yourself with strength. That's fearless identity.

Final Thoughts

The love of God is not just theology or theory—it's meant to be the most intimate, unshakable truth in your life. When you know you are loved, you walk in fearless identity. You live differently. You speak with authority. You stand firm in trials.

This isn't about hype or spiritual performance. It's about revelation. And that revelation leads to declaration. Declaration leads to application. And application leads to transformation.

You are not a victim of your past or your emotions. You are not the sum of others' opinions. You are the beloved workmanship of God, handcrafted with purpose and called to live fearlessly.

Call to Action

Today, choose to declare truth over yourself. Don't wait to feel it. Don't wait for someone else to affirm it. Look in the mirror and speak what God says about you. Declare, "I am the beloved of God. I am fearfully and wonderfully made. I am the workmanship of Christ." When lies creep in, answer them with truth. When fear rises, confront it with love. Let the Word of God be your foundation. Build your identity on His voice alone. Let this be the day you stop striving and start living from the fullness of His love.

Scriptures Referenced

- 1 John 4:19
- 1 John 4:17
- Romans 8:29-30
- Ephesians 2:10
- 2 Corinthians 8:9
- Song of Solomon 6:3
- Romans 8:28
- Romans 8:31
- 1 John 4:18
- Ephesians 2:8-9
- Psalm 139:13-14
- Romans 12:2

Chapter Seven

Blessed Assurance

We're going to continue talking about God's love in this chapter because, honestly, it's something the Lord keeps bringing me back to again and again. No matter how much I study, how many times I teach it, God's love is just that deep, that life-changing, and that foundational.

I remember watching my husband the first time he got a revelation of grace. Scriptures he had always read—ones he had tried to live by in his own strength—suddenly came alive to him. It was like he had been handed a new lens. "Oh, wait, that means this over in Romans... and this in Ephesians!" It was so exciting to see. And while I'd grown up in a church that taught grace, had gone to Bible school, and had been discipled in these truths, I realized I had become a little too familiar with them. The Holy Spirit whispered to my heart, "Then where's your passion?"

That hit me hard. I had to confront the fact that I had grown numb to the very truths that once made the gospel come alive in me. And one of those truths is the love of God. I believe that as we dive into this today, the Holy Spirit is going to stir something inside of you. You're going to see the Word in a new way. This isn't just about knowing God loves you—it's about living like it.

The Transforming Power

There is something about God's love that changes absolutely everything. It's not just a concept or a theological point to understand—it's the very heartbeat of who God is. And when we truly grasp it, it awakens something inside us.

I've seen this over and over again, not just in my husband, but in myself and others. When the revelation of grace and love clicks, the Bible comes alive. It's no longer just words or rules—it becomes a relationship. We begin to see our identity, freedom, authority, and purpose in a whole new light.

But here's the thing: we can get familiar. We can start to skim over foundational truths like "God loves me" and treat them like beginner-level Christianity. But this love? This is everything. We don't graduate from it. We go deeper into it.

God's love is the foundation that everything else stands on. It is the power that renews our minds, heals our wounds, and changes our desires. And when that love takes root, you start to see the fruit in your life. You forgive more easily. You dream bigger. You stand stronger. And most of all, you rest in the assurance that He's for you.

Living Like You're Loved

I was running on the treadmill one morning, listening to a worship song, and the lyrics hit me: "Go ahead and live like you're loved. Go ahead and act like you've been set free. He's giving you more than enough." And I thought, *Yes! That's exactly what God wants for us. He wants us to live like we're loved.*

But how many of us walk around defined by rejection or the shame of our past? We live under other people's opinions or our own failures. That's not what we were meant for.

The enemy works hard to keep us from understanding God's love because once we get it—really get it—we live differently. We walk in freedom. We start to radiate the love we've received.

Now, some might say, "Well, if God loves me no matter what, I can just do whatever I want." But that's not how it works. If that's your response, you haven't really understood the love of God. Because true love transforms you. It changes what you desire. It shifts your entire perspective.

When you live like you're loved, you're not trying to earn approval. You're living from a place of acceptance.

Identity Through Revelation

Our identity is one of the most powerful things we will ever discover in our relationship with God—and the truth is, it's all wrapped up in His love. If we don't understand how deeply we are loved by Him, we will struggle to understand who we are. Because identity doesn't come from what we do; it flows from who God says we are.

And the amazing thing is, He doesn't wait until we have it all figured out to speak identity over us. He doesn't wait for our performance to catch up to His promises. No, He declares truth over us right now—in our process, in our questions, and even in our mess.

I've always loved the Word. I'm kind of a Bible geek—I'll admit it! There's nothing like a good, broken-in Bible, full of highlights, underlines, notes in the margins, and tear-stained pages. I have a preaching Bible, and I have a newer one I'm still breaking in. And to me, there's no better smell in the world than a brand-new Bible. But as much as I love the pages, it's not about the paper and ink—it's about what the Word reveals.

The Scriptures declare who I am. And I don't just mean that they inspire me or give me hope—though they absolutely do. I mean that these verses declare my *spiritual DNA*. They call out my God-given identity. And when I read the Word, I'm not reading wishes—I'm reading reality. I'm reading declarations straight from the heart of God.

So many times, we read a verse and think, *Someday this will be true of me*. We highlight it and write in the margin, "*Claiming this!*" And while it's good to have faith, I want to tell you something: these promises aren't just for "someday." They're for *right now*. You don't need to wait until you've got everything together to walk in who God says you are.

He doesn't love some future, cleaned-up version of you. He loves *you*. Today. Right now. In the middle of whatever you're walking through.

And when we read the Word through the lens of God's love, we stop seeing it as a set of unreachable standards and start seeing it as a mirror of our true identity. This is who you *already are* in Christ. Not who you're hoping to become. Not who you're pretending to be. Not who you're striving to measure up to. But who you already are—because He said so.

Ephesians 1:4-5 gives us a stunning glimpse into this:

> *He chose us in him before the foundation of the world, that we should be holy and blameless before him. In love he predestined us for adoption to himself as sons through Jesus Christ, according to the purpose of His will* (*ESV*).

There it is—your identity, wrapped up in love and chosen *before* you ever did a single thing. Before the world began, God said, "*That one is Mine.*" He didn't choose you for what you could do for Him. He chose you *because He loves you.*

And out of that love, He declared you holy, blameless, adopted, chosen. That's not a slogan—it's your birthright in Christ.

But the enemy works overtime to disconnect us from that truth. He'll try to convince you that your identity is based on your mistakes, your past, your performance, or your circumstances. He'll use your insecurities, your failures, and even the opinions of others to distort the truth about who you are.

And if we don't know what God says, we'll believe whatever lie shouts the loudest.

That's why being in the Word is so essential—it's where the Holy Spirit teaches us our identity. Every time I open my Bible, I'm not just reading—I'm listening. I'm listening for who God says I am. And I don't always get it right away. Sometimes a verse will stir something in my spirit, and I'll write it out in my journal, asking, "*Lord, what does this mean for me?*" And as I sit with it, the Holy Spirit begins to reveal layers of truth that go beyond the surface.

For example, one of the declarations that's changed the way I view myself is this: "I am not trying to become loved—I *am* loved."

It's a subtle shift, but it's everything. I'm not earning God's affection. I'm not convincing Him to choose me. I'm living from a place of being already accepted, already called, and already filled with His Spirit.

That's identity.

And when that revelation drops from your head to your heart, it changes how you show up in the world. You stop shrinking back. You stop comparing. You stop performing for approval. You start walking in boldness—not arrogance, but confidence rooted in His love.

You start saying things like:

- "I am a child of God."
- "I am seated with Christ in heavenly places."
- "I have been given strength and purpose."
- "I am the righteousness of God in Christ Jesus."

These aren't positive affirmations—they're spiritual truths. You're not declaring them to make them true. You're declaring them *because* they're already true.

And here's the beautiful part: when you live from your true identity, you become unshakable. The storms may still come.

Criticism may still sting. Failure may still happen. But none of it changes who you are in Him. You are loved. You are chosen. You are accepted.

If I could encourage you to do one thing consistently, it would be this: open your Bible and ask the Holy Spirit to reveal your identity through the Word. Write down the verses that speak to you. Declare them out loud. And when the lies come—and they will—use those declarations as your sword.

Because the more you hear the truth, the more you'll start to believe it. And when you believe it, you'll start to live it.

That is what it means to live from your identity in God's love. You're not performing for approval—you're living from belonging.

Chosen, Holy, and Blameless in Christ

Let me share a powerful declaration with you from Ephesians 1:4: "*Just as He chose us in Him before the foundation of the world, that we should be holy and blameless before Him in love*" (*Legacy Standard Bible*).

This verse has become so much more than just words on a page for me. For a long time, I read it and felt pressure. I interpreted it through a performance lens: "Okay, God, you chose me, so now I've got to prove that I'm worth choosing. I've got to become holy and blameless so I don't disappoint You."

That's a heavy weight to carry.

But I was missing something crucial—those last two words: "*in love.*"

This wasn't a demand. It was a declaration. It wasn't a checklist. It was a gift. He chose me *in love*. He made me holy and blameless *in love*. It had nothing to do with my perfection and everything to do with His nature.

And this wasn't a last-minute decision. Scripture says He chose us *before the foundation of the world*. That means before you ever made a mistake, before you ever doubted, before you ever took your first breath—He had already made up His mind about you.

You were not a reluctant rescue. You were not a divine afterthought. You were chosen *on purpose*, *with purpose*, and *in love*.

That phrase—*holy and blameless*—used to feel so intimidating. I'd think, *How could I ever be either of those things?* But then the Holy Spirit started to show me something. God's idea of holiness isn't just about external behavior. It's about being set apart. It's about being seen through the lens of Jesus.

When the Father looks at you, He doesn't see your sin or your past. He sees His Son. He sees the blood of Jesus that covers you completely. He sees the righteousness that was exchanged for your brokenness. That's what makes you holy. That's what makes you blameless.

We often think of blame as a verdict—a label we carry because of what we've done. Maybe you've blamed yourself for your kids' struggles. For your marriage falling apart. For missed opportunities or failed businesses. And the enemy is quick to pile on—whispering, "See? That's your fault. That's who you are."

But here's the truth: in Christ, the blame has been removed.

There's no blame in the presence of love.

That's what Paul is saying in Ephesians. You're not working toward holiness—you're living from it. You're not trying to clean yourself up before entering God's presence—you're stepping in because love already made a way.

Let's talk about the word chosen—"*He chose us in Him...*" For some people, that's hard to believe. Especially if they've spent a lifetime being rejected. Maybe people have walked away from you. Maybe you've felt overlooked or invisible. Maybe you've fought to prove your worth, to be accepted, only to end up feeling like you don't measure up.

But the Word says you were chosen: not just tolerated, not picked last, not barely included. You were hand-selected by God Himself.

And not just chosen—but chosen *to be holy and blameless*. That means He didn't pick you because of your potential to get it right. He picked you, knowing everything about you: your strengths, your weaknesses, your past, your future. And He still said, "*I choose you.*"

That kind of love melts away striving.

I want to be really honest with you. For years, I loved God sincerely, but I kept trying to be someone He could use. I thought if I could just reach some level of blamelessness, He would finally trust me with purpose. But that's not how it works. God doesn't wait for you to earn His approval—He clothes you in righteousness the moment you believe.

This frees us from comparison too. Because when we understand we've been chosen in love, we stop measuring ourselves against other people's callings, platforms, or personalities. We begin to walk confidently in who God made *us* to be.

One of the lies the enemy whispers is, "You're too much of a mess to be holy. Too broken to be used. Too flawed to be loved." But God's Word says the opposite. It says you've been made holy, declared blameless, and chosen before time began.

What would your life look like if you really believed that? How would your thoughts change? Your prayers? Your posture?

Here's what I've discovered: when I wake up and declare, "Lord, thank You that I am chosen, holy, and blameless before You in love," it changes the entire trajectory of my day. I don't strive. I don't shrink back. I simply walk in what's already mine.

Friend, you are not working *for* identity. You are living *from* identity. And that identity is this: You are chosen. You are holy. You are blameless. And it's all because of love.

Freedom from Perfectionism and Self-Striving

Growing up, I had this deep, internal need to be perfect. Nobody explicitly told me I had to be, but I just took it on. I was the oldest of six kids in a homeschool family living in a small town, and we were definitely known for being "different." We went to *that* church—you know, the Bible-believing, tongue-talking, miracle-praying kind of church—and people didn't always know what to do with us.

I laugh now when I remember the rumors—people saying we swung from chandeliers. I mean, we didn't, but if we had, it would've been awesome!

But underneath all the fun and faith, I was holding onto this silent burden: *Be perfect, Carrie. Don't mess up. Don't ruin the witness. Don't let anyone down.* And because I genuinely loved God from an early age, that perfectionism got tangled up in my devotion. I thought striving was the same thing as being faithful.

I became my own taskmaster. I set impossible expectations for myself and then held myself accountable when I couldn't meet them. I'd obsess over every word, every choice, every mistake. And over time, I began to carry shame—not just for things I did, but for not doing enough of what I thought I *should* be doing.

Maybe you've been there. Maybe you're there right now.

You're doing all the "right" things—reading your Bible, going to church, serving—but inside, you're exhausted. You're carrying a silent checklist of what you think it means to be a "real Christian," and no matter how many boxes you check, it never feels like enough.

Perfectionism is a cruel master. And the most deceptive part is that it can masquerade as holiness.

I remember thinking, *Well, at least I'm not doing what they're doing. At least I don't struggle with that.* And just like that, pride would creep in. That religious, Pharisee-like attitude—where instead of resting in grace, I started measuring myself and others by performance.

That's when I realized the enemy was attacking me from both sides: if I failed, I was filled with guilt and shame. And if I succeeded, I was tempted with pride and comparison. Either way, it kept me focused on *me*—what I was doing or not doing—instead of on Christ and what He had already done.

But here's the truth that set me free: God is not asking us to strive for perfection—He's asking us to trust in His perfection.

The gospel is not about self-improvement. It's not about behavior modification. It's about transformation through love. And that transformation begins when we lay down our striving and receive His grace.

One of the most healing revelations in my journey was this: God is not shocked by my humanity.

Let that sink in.

He knows my weaknesses. He knows my flaws. He knows my inconsistencies. And still—He loves me, chooses me, and uses me. Not because I'm flawless, but because He is faithful.

There was a season where I constantly felt like I was disappointing God. I'd get so frustrated with myself—*Why can't I just get it together? Why do I still struggle with this? Why do I keep making the same mistake?* And then one day, the Holy Spirit said something so simple and freeing: "Carrie, you're not disappointing Me. You were never holding Me up."

Wow. That wrecked me—in the best way.

God doesn't need us to be perfect. He's not looking for flawless vessels. He's looking for surrendered hearts.

The truth is, your worst day doesn't disqualify you from God's love, and your best day doesn't earn you more of it. His love is not performance-based. It's covenant-based. It's rooted in the unchanging nature of who He is, not the fluctuating reality of what we do.

I want to speak to the version of you that's tired. The you that's been trying so hard for so long. The one who lies awake replaying mistakes. The one who dreads messing up tomorrow. Friend, God's love is not a reward for perfection. It's a refuge for the weary.

You don't have to strive to be worthy. You already are—because of Jesus.

And let's talk about what that means practically. It means when you mess up, you don't run *from* God—you run *to* Him. It means you can be honest in prayer. You don't have to perform. You can say, "Lord, I'm struggling." And He doesn't recoil—He draws near.

I've found that some of the most intimate moments I've had with the Lord weren't when I felt strong, but when I was at my weakest and finally let Him love me there.

And the more you let God love you in your mess, the more your mess starts to lose its power. The love of God doesn't just comfort—it transforms. It doesn't just say, "I forgive you," it says, "Let Me help you walk free."

Now, I'm not saying we just live sloppy, careless lives. Grace doesn't make holiness irrelevant—it makes it possible. But the pursuit of holiness is not about striving for God's approval. It's the natural fruit of receiving His love.

There is rest in grace. There is rest in knowing that the God who called you is also the One who will complete the work in you. You are not a project He regrets. You are a masterpiece in progress.

So, breathe. Lay down the heavy expectations. Let go of the mental checklist. Let God rewrite your definition of "enough."

Because in Christ—you already are.

Adoption and Sonship

Let's talk about something that gets right to the core of who we are—our adoption in Christ. Ephesians 1:5 says it so clearly:

> *He predestined us for adoption as sons through Jesus Christ, according to the purpose of His will* (*English Standard Version Anglicised*).

This verse isn't just a sweet sentiment. It's a bold declaration of our spiritual identity. You weren't randomly swept into God's family. You weren't a last-minute addition. You were *predestined*—hand-selected and intentionally chosen by the Father. And He didn't just choose you for forgiveness. He chose you for family.

And here's the amazing part: God didn't adopt you reluctantly. It wasn't like, "Well, I guess I'll take them too." No, He adopted you with full knowledge of your flaws, your personality quirks, your weaknesses, and your history. And He still said, "I want that one. That one's mine."

That kind of love is overwhelming.

Now, adoption was a concept I had learned about in church, but it became personal when I started seeing it through the lens of sonship—not just being accepted by God but *belonging* to Him. There's a difference between being let in and being brought close. Adoption is about being brought close—into His heart, His inheritance, His household.

I once heard a story about two sisters—one adopted and one biological—who got into an argument. The biological sister said, "Well, at least I'm not adopted." And the adopted sister replied, "Yeah, well, Mom and Dad *had* to take you. They *chose* me."

That might be a little sassier than what Paul meant in Ephesians, but the heart of it is so true. Adoption speaks of being wanted. It says, "You are not a burden. You're not a project. You are a joy."

God chose you. Not out of obligation, but out of love.

I've ministered in countries where adoption is rare or even frowned upon, and I've seen how radical this truth is for people. In many cultures, being adopted is seen as second-class. But in the kingdom of God, adoption is **elevated**. It's not a lesser status—it's a divine one.

And Paul uses the term adoption very intentionally. In Roman law, when someone was adopted into a family, they were given full legal rights. They weren't treated like outsiders—they were treated like heirs. In fact, an adopted child in that culture couldn't be disowned. It was permanent, secure, and final.

And that's exactly what God is communicating to us: *You are Mine, and nothing is going to change that.*

As I've grown in my understanding of God's love, I've come to see adoption not just as a theological concept but as an anchor for my soul. Because let's be honest, life has a way of making us feel rejected—maybe by people, by institutions, or even by ourselves.

But our adoption in Christ silences every lie of rejection.

When you feel overlooked, remind yourself—"I've been adopted." When you feel unworthy, remind yourself—"I've been chosen." When you feel like an outsider, remind yourself—"I've been brought in."

Adoption brings with it more than just identity—it brings **inheritance**. Romans 8 tells us we are co-heirs with Christ (Rom. 8:17). That means everything that belongs to Him belongs to us. His righteousness. His authority. His peace. His purpose.

Let that sink in for a minute. You are not spiritually bankrupt. You are an heir. You have access to everything you need—not because you earned it, but because you were adopted into it.

And here's where I want to speak specifically to some of you who have wrestled with father wounds or family rejection. Maybe you've never known the stability of a father's love. Maybe your earthly experience has distorted your view of God. I get that. I've walked with people who've had to untangle painful histories just to begin trusting God as Father.

But let me say this gently and boldly: God is not like the people who hurt you.

He is faithful. He is present. He is kind. He doesn't walk away when you mess up. He doesn't pull back when you question things. He doesn't withhold affection until you perform. He is a good Father. And He adopted you not just to change your status—but to heal your heart.

And the healing often begins when we stop trying to earn sonship and start receiving it.

This identity changes how we pray. I don't come to God like a beggar—I come like a daughter. I don't wonder if He's listening—I know I have His ear. I don't plead for scraps—I expect abundance because I'm at His table.

I remember one morning, just sitting with the Lord during my quiet time, journaling about things that were on my heart—dreams, burdens, questions—and I felt the Holy Spirit whisper, "You don't have to strive for My attention. You already have My affection." That broke me—in the best way.

I don't have to prove that I belong. I already do. That's adoption.

So, if you've been feeling distant, uncertain, or unworthy, I encourage you—lean into this truth: You are a child of God. You have been adopted in love. And your Father delights in you.

You don't have to knock on the door and ask to come in. You're already home.

Strength and Purpose Through Christ

Let's talk about purpose for a moment—not just the idea of having one, but the confidence to *walk in it*. And not in your own strength, but in the strength that comes from Christ.

This verse from 1 Timothy 1:12 has meant so much to me, especially in seasons when I felt unqualified or unsure:

> *I thank Christ Jesus our Lord, who has given me strength, that he considered me trustworthy, appointing me to his service* (*NIV*).

I can't even count how many times I've returned to this Scripture. It's not just a verse I quote—it's a reminder of how God thinks about us. He gives us strength. He considers us trustworthy. He appoints us—not because we earned it but because He sees something in us that we often overlook: *His own nature.*

When I first stepped into ministry, I was just twenty-one years old and newly on the mission field in Russia. I felt so young, so inexperienced. I believed in the call, but everything in me felt inadequate. I didn't know how to lead. I didn't know how to "be a missionary." But I knew one thing—I loved the Word.

And every time I opened it during that season, the Lord brought me back to First and Second Timothy. Every day, for two years, I tried to read other passages, but He kept saying, "Go back." And eventually, He let me read Titus too—but even that was part of the lesson. God was teaching me how to walk in strength, not in my own abilities but in His Spirit.

This verse—"[He] *has given me strength*"—became my lifeline. It taught me that strength is not something I muster up. It's something He deposits in me. It's not tied to how confident I feel or how capable I look. It's based entirely on who He is *in me*.

And here's the beautiful thing: God doesn't just give strength; He assigns purpose. The verse continues, "*He considered me trustworthy, appointing me to His service.*"

That line wrecked me. Because I had always thought I had to prove myself to God. Like maybe if I was good enough, faithful enough, consistent enough, *then* He'd give me something to do. But that's not what Paul is saying. God doesn't appoint you after you've proven yourself—He appoints you *because He sees you through the lens of grace.*

He considered me trustworthy. He *judged* me faithful. And that doesn't mean I had a flawless track record. It means He saw Himself in me. He saw what His Spirit could accomplish through my surrender.

When God looks at you, He doesn't see just your weaknesses or limitations. He sees Jesus. He sees the finished work of the cross. He sees His own Spirit dwelling inside you. And based on that, He says, "I trust you with this."

Isn't that amazing? That the God of the universe looks at us—not through a lens of failure, but through the lens of redemption—and says, "I can use that one."

And I want to say this directly to you: God has given you strength. He has called you. And He considers you trustworthy.

Maybe you've doubted that. Maybe you've thought, *Sure, God can use others—but not me. I'm too weak. Too broken. Too ordinary*. But that's not what He says.

In fact, Scripture tells us that His power is made perfect in weakness. That means the very thing you think disqualifies you might be the very area where His strength shines the brightest.

One of the things we say all the time at Charis Bible College is this: *God wants you to find, follow, and fulfill the call of God on your life*. And it's true. He doesn't just want to reveal your purpose—He wants to equip you to walk in it.

But here's where many of us get stuck. We may find the call, maybe even feel excited about it for a moment, but we struggle to follow it. Why? Because the enemy starts whispering lies: "You're not ready. You're not spiritual enough. You missed your chance. Someone else could do it better."

And those lies keep us sidelined.

But let me tell you—God hasn't changed His mind about you.

Even if you've delayed obedience, made mistakes, or have been running in the opposite direction, His strength hasn't run out. His calling is still secure. The gifts and callings of God are irrevocable.

When I read that He has *appointed me to His service*, it reminds me that this calling is personal. It's not just ministry on a platform. It's the calling to be a mother, a spouse, a friend, a light in my workplace, a mentor, a listener, and a leader in whatever sphere I'm placed.

And I want to encourage you—don't devalue your calling just because it doesn't look like someone else's.

Sometimes people come to me and say, "Carrie, I feel like I'm just a mom," or "I'm just running a business. I'm not doing anything big for God." But let me tell you—raising children to know and love the Lord is no small purpose. Starting a business that reflects the heart and integrity of God is no small assignment.

There is no such thing as a small calling when it comes from a big God.

And whatever season you're in, it matters. Maybe right now your assignment looks like changing diapers and doing school drop-off. Maybe it's clocking in and out of a job that feels mundane. Maybe it's caregiving or starting over.

But if God has called you to it, He's also equipped you for it.

Let me also encourage those of you who feel like God isn't speaking right now. I've had people come to me and say, "I'm reading my Bible, I'm fasting, I'm worshiping—but I can't hear Him." And often, the question I'll ask is: "What's the last thing He told you? Did you do it?"

Sometimes, we're looking for a new word when God is still waiting for obedience to the last one. And here's what I've learned: obedience is not burdensome when you know you're loved. When you understand that He has called you *in love*, obedience becomes a joy—not a job.

So, if you've been waiting for perfect circumstances, the right timing, or a certain level of "spiritual maturity" before you step into your purpose—stop waiting. Say yes now. Trust the strength He's given you. Trust that He knows what He's doing.

Because He *has* appointed you, and He considers you trustworthy.

Hearing God's Voice and Obeying from Love

One of the questions I get asked more than almost anything else is this: "Carrie, how do I hear God's voice?"

People will come to me after a teaching on God's love or identity, and they're so hungry. They say, "I want to experience that kind of relationship with God. I want to hear Him like that. Will you pray that I get that kind of revelation too?"

And my answer is always "yes—I'll absolutely pray for you." But I also want to tell people the truth, because I think we sometimes over-spiritualize what hearing from God is supposed to feel like. We imagine a booming voice, a vision, or an emotional experience. But more often than not, revelation comes in the quiet, consistent pursuit of Him—especially through the Word.

I didn't have one big "burning bush" moment where everything suddenly clicked. For me, it came over years of simply sitting with the Word, journaling, asking questions, listening, writing down thoughts, and inviting the Holy Spirit to speak to me through it all. And He did.

As a little girl, I remember walking around with my Bible in Sunday school and saying, "Someday, I'm going to preach this!" I didn't fully understand what I was saying, but I knew this Word was powerful. And so even as a teenager, especially when we started homeschooling, I would spend hours with my Bible—reading, underlining, asking the Lord to help me understand.

That's how I began to hear His voice—not through hype or noise but through the quiet, steady, daily pursuit of truth.

And even now, I still approach the Word with expectation. I'll open up my Bible in the morning, but I also keep my journal and my Day-Timer nearby. Why? Because as soon as I start reading, the enemy loves to throw distractions at me. *Oh no, I forgot to take the chicken out for dinner! Oh! I was supposed to respond to that email.*

So, instead of jumping up or grabbing my phone, I just write those things down in my Day-Timer, park them there, and go right back to the Word. I'm not going to let the devil steal the time I've set apart to hear from God. That simple habit has helped me stay focused and keep my heart tuned in to what the Holy Spirit wants to say.

Now, let me tell you something else that's really important when it comes to hearing God's voice: God doesn't stop speaking. But sometimes we stop listening because we haven't obeyed the last thing He said.

As mentioned before, I can't count how many times I've had someone say to me, "Carrie, I've been praying, fasting, and worshipping, but I still don't feel like I'm hearing from the Lord." And my response is often, "What's the last thing He told you? Did you do it?"

There's usually a pause. And then they'll say, "Well, God told me to do this, but I haven't done it yet because..." And they'll list all the reasons why it wasn't the right time, or they didn't feel ready, or they were waiting for confirmation.

But here's the thing: obedience opens the door to deeper revelation.

If we haven't responded to the last thing He said, why would He skip ahead to the next part? God isn't withholding His voice or playing hard to get. He's neither distant nor punishing us for missing it. But He is consistent. He speaks with purpose.

It's like being in a boat with Jesus, and He's giving you directions: "Row in this direction." But instead, you keep trying to go the other way. And then you say, "Lord, why aren't You saying anything new?" He's like, "Because I already told you, and I'm not going to change My mind."

Now hear me—this isn't about guilt. It's about trust. God wants to lead you. But He leads those who are willing to follow. That's why obedience is so powerful—it aligns us with His direction and opens us to hear more clearly.

But here's the key: Obedience must be rooted in love.

If you try to obey God out of fear, duty, or pressure, it becomes religion. It becomes striving. It becomes a heavy burden. But when obedience flows from a revelation of love, it becomes a joy.

Jesus said, "*If you love me, you will keep my commandments*" (John 14:15, *ESV*). That wasn't a threat. It was a natural outcome. When you know how deeply He loves you, obedience becomes a response of love, not a requirement to earn it.

That's why I talk so much about the love of God—because without that foundation, we'll always misinterpret His voice. We'll hear correction as condemnation. We'll hear instruction as pressure. But when you know He loves you—really, deeply loves you—you start to hear Him differently. You hear His guidance as protection, His promptings as care, and His commands as invitations to walk with Him in freedom.

I've had moments where I resisted something God was telling me to do. Not because I didn't believe it was Him, but because it was uncomfortable. It required stretching. And sometimes, I just didn't feel ready. But every single time I obeyed—even if it felt awkward, even if it felt costly—I found grace waiting on the other side. I found joy I couldn't have anticipated. I found breakthrough I didn't know I needed.

God's not looking for perfect obedience. He's looking for surrendered hearts.

So, if you've been wondering why you can't seem to hear Him right now, maybe it's time to go back to the last thing He said. Ask Him again. Revisit that word, that prompt, that call. And don't approach it like a burden. Let love lead you.

God isn't just trying to get you to do something for Him—He's trying to walk with you. He's trying to show you who He is, how deeply He cares, and how good His plans are for your life.

And as you walk with Him, step by step, day by day, you'll find yourself not only hearing His voice more clearly—but obeying more freely. Not because you have to, but because you *want* to.

Final Thoughts

If there's one thing I pray you walk away with from this chapter, it's this: you are deeply, unshakably, eternally loved by God. Not in theory, not just in principle, but in reality—right now. Wherever you are, whatever your past looks like, however you feel about yourself today—He loves you.

And that love changes everything.

It changes how you live. When you understand God's love, you don't walk around in shame or fear. You begin to live like you're loved. Not in arrogance but in confidence. Not trying to prove yourself to the world but resting in the assurance that *you already belong*.

It changes how you think. His love becomes the lens through which you view your identity. You're not what you've done. You're not what others have said. You are who He says you are—chosen, holy, blameless, and adopted as His own.

It changes how you relate to God. You're not working your way toward Him. You're not begging for scraps of approval. You're a son. You're a daughter. You've been brought close—not because you performed, but because Jesus made a way. You've been given access to the Father—not as a servant hoping for favor but as a child already favored.

And His love changes how you obey. You don't serve God to earn His love—you serve because you *have* His love. You don't follow Him to prove your worth—you follow Him because you *know* your worth. That's what makes obedience light and joyful instead of heavy and exhausting. Obedience becomes your "yes" to the One who already said "yes" to you at the cross.

This love changes how you approach your calling. Maybe you've doubted whether God could use someone like you. Maybe you've compared your life to others and decided your purpose is too small or that you're too late. But God doesn't see you through the lens of human potential—He sees you through the finished work of Jesus. And based on that, He says, "*I can trust you with My purposes.*" You've been given strength. You've been appointed. You are trustworthy—not because of your record, but because of your Redeemer.

And friend, this love even changes how you hear His voice. It silences the lies of the enemy and tunes your heart to the whispers of the Spirit. It takes you out of striving and into surrender. You don't have to fight for God's attention. You already have it. You don't have to wonder if you're worthy to hear from Him. He's already speaking—you just need to trust that love has opened your ears.

So, if you've been striving—striving to be enough, striving to be perfect, striving to earn your place—it's time to lay all that down. Let love do the heavy lifting. Let grace rewrite your definition of success. Let your identity be rooted not in what you do but in whose you are.

You are loved.
You are chosen.
You are holy and blameless in Christ.
You are adopted.
You are strong.
You are appointed.

You are trustworthy.
And you are deeply known by a God who is not disappointed in you—but delighted in you.

That is what gives us blessed assurance. Not our perfection but His promises. Not our striving but His sufficiency. Not our strength but His grace. Not our love for Him—but His unstoppable, unchanging, and unwavering love for us.

Call to Action

Take a moment today—right where you are—and pause. Not to perform. Not to prove anything. But simply to say: "Lord, I receive Your love."

Let that be your starting place. Let it be your daily place. Lay down the striving. Lay down the mental checklist. Let go of the idea that you have to earn something that was already purchased at the cross. Instead, receive the truth that you are chosen, holy, blameless, adopted, strengthened, and appointed—because of Jesus.

Maybe you've been stuck in perfectionism. Maybe you've been carrying the weight of trying to "get it right" before stepping into your purpose. Or maybe you've been waiting for a sign, thinking you have to feel more qualified before you can move forward.

Friend, you don't need to wait any longer.
You don't need to clean yourself up before God can use you.

You don't need to hear a new word—just say yes to the last one.

Open the Word and ask the Holy Spirit to show you who you are through His eyes. Keep your journal nearby. Keep your Bible open. Write out the declarations that speak to your identity and inheritance. And when distractions come—and they will—write them down, park them, and return to the Word.

Invite the Holy Spirit to teach you. Let Him guide you into truth. Let Him be the one who shows you just how deeply you are loved—not once, not occasionally, but *every day*.

Say yes to your calling.
Say yes to rest.
Say yes to walking in the strength He's already given you.
Say yes to hearing His voice and following it—not out of pressure, but out of love.

Because when you live from love, everything changes.

This is your moment to stop striving and start walking. You are loved. You are called. You are ready—because He is with you.

Scriptures Referenced

- Ephesians 1:4
- Ephesians 1:5
- 1 Timothy 1:12
- Romans 8:17

Chapter Eight

Stay Hungry

I have walked with the Lord for many, many years—since I was six years old, and Spirit-filled by the time I was seven. And I can say without hesitation: there is always more. The longer I walk with God, the more I realize how much deeper His love goes, how much wider His truth stretches, and how unending His goodness truly is. Just when I think I understand something—just when I think, *Oh, I've got a revelation of that!*—God opens up even more. That's the beauty of our relationship with Him. He's too big, too good, too generous to ever be fully contained by a single moment of insight.

In this chapter, we're going to talk about what it means to stay spiritually hungry—to keep coming back for more of God's presence, His Word, and His love. We'll explore how the enemy tries to shrink our appetite, distract our hearts, and twist the truth of God's love. But more importantly, we'll see how the love of God reshapes our understanding of value, expands our desire for Him, and empowers us to live boldly, obediently, and full of trust.

This is an invitation to feast. Not just once but daily. Not just with obligation but with joy. Let's dig into what it means to *stay hungry*.

There's Always More

When you've known the Lord for decades, you start to see a pattern. You think you've arrived at a solid understanding—maybe you've had a powerful moment where something clicks deep inside you—and then God shows you there's another level. That's not a sign of immaturity. That's a sign of intimacy.

God always takes it deeper. He continues to reveal His heart in new ways, not because He's holding out on us, but because He's so big, so good, and so full of truth that we could never exhaust Him. That's what keeps the hunger alive in our relationship with Him.

Paul captured this desire in his letter to the Philippians when he said:

> *Indeed, I count everything as loss because of the surpassing worth of knowing Christ Jesus my Lord. For his sake I have suffered the loss of all things and count them as rubbish, in order that I may gain Christ.*
>
> Philippians 3:8, *ESV*

That's the shift in perspective the love of God brings. We begin to recognize what's of *real value*. The things of this world start to lose their grip because we've tasted something better. Our view of success, fulfillment, even identity, gets recalibrated by the eternal weight of knowing Jesus.

The Bible says in Proverbs 4:18:

> *But the path of the righteous is like the light of dawn, which shines brighter and brighter until full day* (*ESV*).

That's what your relationship with God looks like. Brighter and brighter. Deeper and deeper. There's always more. That's why spiritual hunger isn't a burden—it's a blessing. It's proof that your spirit is alive and connected to the source of all life.

And how do you grow that hunger? You eat. Just like in the natural, your appetite expands the more you feed it. When Mike and I travel internationally for ministry—whether we're at a Charis school in Switzerland or a seminar in Africa—we always eat well. Breakfast, lunch, and even those late-night student meals after teaching! At first, we think we're stuffed. But the next morning, we're ready for more. Why? Because we've stretched our stomachs with consistent nourishment.

It's the same with your soul. Feed it the Word. Feed it worship. Feed it the presence of God. At first, you may feel satisfied—but give it a moment, and you'll be hungry again. That's the beauty of the Bread of Life. The more you partake of Jesus, the more your desire for Him grows.

So don't be discouraged if you feel like your appetite is small right now. Just start eating. Just show up. The Holy Spirit knows how to awaken your hunger. And what He reveals will change everything.

The Enemy Perverts What God Meant for Good

From the beginning, the enemy has made it his mission to twist the truth of God's love. He perverts anything God made—especially the Gospel. He doesn't come with blatant opposition. He comes with subtle distortion, a slight shift in perception, a whisper of doubt. "Did God really say…?"

In Genesis 3:1–5, we see the first perversion of truth:

> *Now the serpent was more crafty than any other beast of the field that the Lord God had made. He said to the woman, "Did God actually say, 'You shall not eat of any tree in the garden'?" And the woman said to the serpent, "We may eat of the fruit of the trees in the garden, but God said, 'You shall not eat of the fruit of the tree that is in the midst of the garden, neither shall you touch it, lest you die.'" But the serpent said to the woman, "You will not surely die. For God knows that when you eat of it your eyes will be opened, and you will be like God, knowing good and evil"* (ESV).

The enemy made it seem like God was holding something back—like He was limiting Adam and Eve, keeping them from a greater life. And that lie—God is withholding something good from you—is still active today.

When I spoke with my daughter during our mother-daughter weekend, we talked openly about God's original design for sex and how the enemy has tried to pervert it. It wasn't a scary conversation—it was Spirit-filled, full of peace and grace. But it underscored something so important: the enemy wants to distort what is beautiful. And when we don't teach the truth, the lies seem louder.

This happens not only in sexuality but in every area of our lives—our identity, our purpose, how we approach God. The enemy even distorts our perception of God's love by whispering, "God will only love you if you stop struggling, if you fix your addiction, if you stop failing." But that is *not* the Gospel.

The Word says in Romans 5:8:

> *But God shows his love for us in that while we were still sinners, Christ died for us* (ESV).

And in James 1:17:

> *Every good gift and every perfect gift is from above, coming down from the Father of lights, with whom there is no variation or shadow due to change* (ESV).

There is no shadow in Him. No withholding. No trick. Just perfect love and perfect gifts. The devil's strategy is always to get you to question the goodness of your Creator.

But when we stay rooted in God's love, we begin to see through the lies. As Jesus said in John 10:10:

> *The thief comes only to steal and kill and destroy. I came that they may have life and have it abundantly* (ESV).

God is not holding anything back from you. In Christ, He gave *everything*. He gave His only Son. He gave righteousness. He gave His Spirit. The enemy wants to shrink your appetite by making you think there's nothing more for you. But God says, "Come and eat. There's more."

God's Love Reveals True Value

One of the most powerful things the love of God does is realign our value system. When we begin to grasp how much we are loved by Him, our perspective shifts. We stop measuring worth by the world's standards, and we begin to see everything through the lens of eternity.

The world is constantly trying to tell us what success looks like, what beauty looks like, what our lives should look like. You need to have this kind of house, this kind of job, this kind of body. And if you don't, you've failed. But here's the catch: the moment you reach one of those goals, the world moves the target. The enemy will always say, "Well, that's not enough. This is what you need now." And so, you're left in a cycle of comparison, dissatisfaction, and hunger for things that never satisfy.

But when you experience the love of God, everything changes. Remember what you just read in Philippians 3:8:

> *Indeed, I count everything as loss because of the surpassing worth of knowing Christ Jesus my Lord. For His sake I have suffered the loss of all things and count them as rubbish, in order that I may gain Christ (ESV).*

What a bold declaration! Paul is saying, "Everything else is trash compared to knowing Jesus." That's not hyperbole. That's a man who had encountered the overwhelming love and worth of God and realized: nothing else compares.

The love of God gives us clarity. It shows us what truly matters—what holds eternal weight—and what is just noise. It frees us from the striving, the proving, the exhausting chase for worldly validation.

This is why Paul also wrote in Philippians 1:9–11:

> *And it is my prayer that your love may abound more and more, with knowledge and all discernment, so that you may approve what is excellent, and so be pure and blameless for the day of Christ, filled with the fruit of righteousness that*

> *comes through Jesus Christ, to the glory and praise of God* (*ESV*).

I love how the *Amplified Bible* puts verse 10:

> *So that you may learn to recognize* and *treasure what is excellent [identifying the best and distinguishing moral differences]; and that you may be pure and blameless until the day of Christ [actually living lives that lead others away from sin].*

That's what the love of God does—it gives you discernment. It helps you recognize what is of *real* value. What is excellent. What is lasting. And it helps you let go of what's worthless.

I've seen this so clearly in my own life. As Mike and I have traveled internationally, planted Bible schools, and watched students around the world come alive to the Word, I've realized that it's not the size of your house or the number of your followers that counts. It's the fruit of righteousness. It's seeing lives changed because you chose to value the Gospel over comfort.

God's love changes how you spend your time, how you pray, how you raise your children, and how you lead your marriage. You begin to say, "Lord, I want what You want. I want what matters to *You*."

And what's amazing is, when you begin to value what God values, you also begin to walk in contentment. Not the kind of contentment that means you settle or stop growing—but the kind that says, "I know who I am. I know what I have in Christ. And that's enough." You're no longer chasing false finish lines. You're rooted.

But here's the beautiful paradox of God's love—it brings both contentment and a deeper hunger. You're content in His presence yet always longing for more of it. That's the mystery Paul spoke of in Ephesians 3:18–19, that we would:

> *...have strength to comprehend with all the saints what is the breadth and length and height and depth, and to know the love of Christ that surpasses knowledge, that you may be filled with all the fullness of God* (*ESV*).

This is what it means to live in God's value system. It means we don't measure our days by accomplishments or applause—we measure them by intimacy. We measure them by knowing Jesus. And when we do, we find that everything else fades in comparison.

Staying Hungry by Feeding Daily

One of the questions I get asked the most is, "Carrie, how do I stay hungry for God?" It's such an honest and important question—and the answer is beautifully simple: you stay hungry by eating.

That's how it works in the natural. In the natural, when you fast, your stomach shrinks. The less you eat, the less hungry you feel. And over time, your appetite diminishes. But when you eat consistently, your body expects nourishment. You develop an appetite. You wake up and think, *What's for breakfast?* Right?

It's the same spiritually. You don't get hungry for God by waiting around for some emotional lightning bolt. You get hungry by feeding on His Word. By listening to His voice. By worshiping Him in spirit and truth. The more you eat, the more your heart desires Him. The more you experience His goodness, the more you crave it.

Psalm 34:8 says,

Taste and see that the Lord is good! Blessed is the man who takes refuge in him! (ESV).

Taste. See. That means *engage* with Him. Don't just admire the banquet from a distance—pull up a chair and dig in.

What happens when you feed daily on God's Word is that you stretch your spiritual appetite. And you find yourself saying, "Lord, I just want more of You. That was good, but I'm still hungry."

The Bible says in Psalm 119:32:

I will run in the way of your commandments when you enlarge my heart! (ESV).

I love that! God's Word *enlarges* your heart. It gives you the capacity to desire more. It creates space for joy, for peace, for power, for revelation.

But here's what the enemy does—he distracts. He gets you busy. He surrounds you with noise. Not necessarily evil things—just noisy things. Urgent emails, social media scrolls, long to-do lists. And slowly, your appetite begins to shrink. You stop prioritizing spiritual nourishment. And before long, your heart feels dry. Unmotivated. Even apathetic.

That's why Paul's words in Philippians 3:8 are so vital. He had learned what was truly valuable—and it wasn't success, status, or stuff. It was Jesus.

And I believe God wants to stir that same pursuit in you. Not just a Sunday morning hunger. Not just a crisis-driven hunger. But a daily, intimate, ongoing craving for more of His presence.

And the beautiful thing is—He's not withholding anything. He's not rationing His love. He's not saying, "I'll give you more once you prove yourself." No, He's saying:

> *Blessed are those who hunger and thirst for righteousness, for they shall be satisfied*
>
> Matthew 5:6, *ESV*

That's a promise. If you hunger for Him, you *will* be filled.

So, if you feel like your appetite has been small lately, that's okay. Don't feel shame. Just start feeding again. Read one verse. Spend five minutes in worship. Ask the Holy Spirit to expand your heart.

Because this is how you stay hungry: you eat, and then you want more. And more. And more. And the more you receive, the more you realize that no other feast compares.

Love Produces Trust, and Trust Produces Obedience

One of the most beautiful and powerful truths I've learned in my walk with the Lord is this: when you know how deeply God loves you, trusting Him becomes easy—and obedience becomes a joy. It's not about forcing yourself to trust. It's about *experiencing His love* in such a real way that you can't help but trust Him.

So many times, people come to me and say, "Carrie, I want to trust God more. I'm struggling to believe what He's asking of me. Do you have any good Scriptures on trust?" And while there are definitely scriptures that talk about trusting the Lord, I usually respond with something that surprises them: "You don't have a trust problem. You have a love problem."

See, trust is the fruit—*love* is the root. When you really know that someone loves you, you don't hesitate to follow their lead. You don't second-guess their motives. You lean in with confidence because you know they have your best in mind.

That's why Psalm 143 became so alive to me when I was meditating on the love of God. Listen to what David says in verses 7–10:

> *Answer me quickly, O LORD! My spirit fails! Hide not your face from me, lest I be like those who go down to the pit. Let me hear in the morning of your steadfast love, for in you I trust. Make me know the way I should go, for to you I lift up my soul. Deliver me from my enemies, O LORD! I have fled to you for refuge. Teach me to do your will, for you are my God! Let your good Spirit lead me on level ground!* (ESV).

There's such intimacy in that passage. David is crying out—not in panic, but in trust. "*Let me hear in the morning of your steadfast love, for in you I trust.*" You see that connection? Because of God's love, David could trust Him. And because he trusted Him, he surrendered his will and asked to be taught and led.

This is the kind of intimacy God wants with each of us. He wants you to wake up in the morning and say, "God, I trust You because I know You love me. I don't have to figure everything out. I don't need all the answers today. I just need to know that You're with me, and You are."

And when you trust Him, your response shifts from hesitation to obedience. Now, I'm not saying obedience is always comfortable. In fact, it often presses up against our flesh and our comfort zones. Sometimes God will ask you to take a step that feels uncertain—like moving to a new city, changing jobs, letting go of a relationship, or forgiving someone who deeply hurt you.

And in those moments, your mind might scream, "This doesn't make sense!" But your spirit, rooted in love, responds, "Yes, Lord. I trust You."

That's where obedience is born. Not out of religious pressure or fear of missing it—but out of *love.*

Jesus said it so simply in John 14:15:

If you love me, you will keep my commandments (ESV).

Obedience isn't about trying harder. It's about loving deeper. And love doesn't come from striving—it comes from surrender. It comes from letting God love you first.

Sometimes I describe it like this—just to paint a bold picture: You know, in a marriage, intimacy comes from transparency, trust, and vulnerability. It's the same in our relationship with the Lord. He has loved us completely—He has given everything for us. Now our response is to love Him back. And how do we do that? *Through obedience.*

We say, "God, I don't understand this, but I know You love me. So, I'm going to follow You. I'm going to do what You said, even if it stretches me. Even if it costs me. Even if it's hard. Because I trust You."

And what's amazing is that on the *other side* of obedience is always testimony. I've never obeyed God and regretted it. Sure, my flesh might have resisted at first. But every single time I've said yes to Him, I've discovered joy, peace, fruitfulness—and a deeper revelation of His love.

You cannot walk with God and not have testimonies. His Word is a seed. When it gets into your heart and you start responding in obedience, it grows. It changes things. It transforms you from the inside out.

So today, don't focus on trying harder to trust or to obey. Focus on receiving His love. Ask Him to show you how much He loves you. Because when that truth hits your heart—when you *know* that you are deeply loved—trust becomes natural, and obedience becomes your love language back to Him.

Obedience Leads to Testimonies and Fruitfulness

Here's something I've learned again and again in walking with the Lord: you cannot walk in obedience to God's Word—motivated by love—and not see fruit. It is impossible. The Word is living, active, and powerful. When you take it in, believe it, and act on it, your life begins to bear witness to His goodness. You start to see testimonies.

That's what I love about the nature of God. He doesn't just give us commands—He leads us into the kind of life that *produces* something. And that fruit, it's not forced. It flows from relationship.

Paul talks about this kind of fruitfulness in Philippians 1:11:

> *Filled with the fruit of righteousness that comes through Jesus Christ, to the glory and praise of God* (ESV).

The righteousness we carry is not something we earn. It's something we *receive*—and once received, it begins to overflow in our lives as obedience, as boldness, as love, as action. And all of it glorifies God.

Obedience is the doorway to testimony. When we obey—*not* to earn God's favor, but because we are already loved—we walk into divine appointments, miracles, and revelations we never could've engineered on our own. And it's not just about *what* you do—it's *why* you do it.

This is what Paul meant when he prayed that our love would abound in knowledge and discernment, so that we would "*approve what is excellent*" (Phil. 1:9–10). When love is our foundation, it shapes our decision-making. It changes how we see people. It impacts how we spend our time and where we place our energy.

And the more we walk in step with the Spirit, the more *fruit* we produce:

> *But the fruit of the Spirit is love, joy, peace, patience, kindness, goodness, faithfulness, gentleness, self-control....*
>
> Galatians 5:22–23, *ESV*

That's the evidence of a heart aligned with God. It's not forced behavior—it's fruit. And it comes when we let God love us and we respond with surrender.

Sometimes, that obedience looks like stepping into something brand new. Other times, it looks like staying faithful in a season where you feel invisible. But either way, when you obey God out of love, *He does something with it.*

I remember during our international ministry travels, walking into situations where the Lord asked us to pour out, to teach, to minister, to serve—even when we were tired, even when it didn't make sense in the moment. But every single time, we came away with stories of healing, breakthrough, and transformation.

And often, those testimonies weren't immediate. Sometimes they came months later—students reaching out to say how their lives changed because of something God said through a message, a prayer, a conversation. That's the fruit of obedience.

It reminds me of Psalm 119:105:

Your word is a lamp to my feet and a light to my path (*ESV*).

We don't always see the full picture when we obey. But His Word lights the next step. And as we keep stepping, a path of fruitfulness unfolds. Our obedience today creates testimonies tomorrow.

And this is what I want to encourage you with: your life *will* produce fruit when it's rooted in God's love. You may not feel it in the moment. You may not see all the evidence yet. But the seed is working. The Spirit is moving. And your faith-filled steps of obedience are leading to breakthrough—not just for you but for the people God's called you to impact.

So, if you're wondering, *Is this worth it?*—yes. Every yes to God, every surrender, every act of obedience—*it matters*. And the fruit will come.

Prayer Becomes a Pursuit

One of the most incredible transformations that happens when you begin to understand God's love is that it completely shifts how you approach Him. You stop praying from a place of fear or desperation, and you start praying from a place of confidence and intimacy. Your prayer life becomes a pursuit—not of performance but of presence.

Let's go back to how David prayed in Psalm 143:8–10. He said:

> *Let me hear in the morning of your steadfast love, for in you I trust. Make me know the way I should go, for to you I lift up my soul. ... Teach me to do your will, for you are my God! Let your good Spirit lead me on level ground!* (ESV).

This prayer carries so much passion and trust. It wasn't just a cry for help; it was a declaration of love and dependence. David was saying, "God, I want to hear You first thing in the morning. I want to be led by Your love. I want to walk in Your will."

And that's what daily pursuit looks like. It's not waking up every day trying to earn God's approval. It's waking up with the deep assurance that *you already have it*. And because of that, you hunger for His voice. You desire His direction.

I've learned that when you start your day with the love of God, everything else shifts. Your priorities change. Your attitude changes. Your confidence grows. Why? Because you're not begging God to show up. You're declaring, "Lord, because You love me, I trust You. I lift up my soul to You. I want to walk in Your way."

This kind of relationship is not about duty—it's about *delight.*

It reminds me of Song of Solomon 2:4, where it says:

> *He brought me to the banqueting house, and his banner over me was love* (*ESV*).

I love that image. God has drawn you into a feast, and He's waving a massive spiritual banner over your life that says, "LOVED." Not just tolerated. Not just forgiven. *Deeply, unconditionally, joyfully loved.*

And when that truth settles into your heart, your pursuit becomes bold. You're not hiding. You're running to Him. You're seeking Him—not because you're afraid of missing it, but because you're drawn by His goodness.

This is the transformation I see in so many students at Charis. At first, they come in hungry but unsure—wondering if they're really qualified to hear God's voice or be used by Him. But as the love of God begins to settle deep into their hearts, something changes. They start praying differently. Not out of striving but out of trust. They start expecting to hear from Him. They begin living from the revelation that they are *already loved.*

And that's what God desires for each of us. He doesn't just want you to know His love on Sundays or during worship. He wants you to wake up every single day and say, "God, thank You for loving me. Show me what You want me to do today. I lift up my heart to You."

This kind of daily pursuit is powerful. It shapes how you respond to life's challenges. It guides how you pray about your family, your job, your future. It fills you with boldness—not arrogance but holy confidence.

Because when you know you're loved, you can face anything. You can pray with authority. You can speak with clarity. You can love others without fear of rejection.

And here's the best part—God *loves* when you pursue Him. He delights when you wake up and the first words out of your mouth are, "Good morning, Lord." You're not trying to twist His arm—you're simply responding to the One who already gave everything for you.

So let your prayers reflect that. Let your pursuit be fueled by love. Ask Him daily, "Lord, what do You want me to do today? What's on Your heart?" Because that kind of pursuit—born out of relationship, not religion—is the kind of life that overflows with purpose, joy, and supernatural fruit.

Love Is Our Refuge and Power in Battle

There's something incredibly powerful that happens when you begin to understand the love of God—not just as a warm, comforting feeling, but as a place of refuge and a source of victory.

Let me tell you something: the love of God is not passive. It's not soft. It's not weak. It is fierce. It is protective. It's a banner raised over your life that declares to the enemy, "You cannot have this one." I keep coming back to these scriptures in Psalms 143 because they are so rich and empowering.

In Psalm 143:9, David writes:

> *Deliver me from my enemies, O Lord! I have fled to you for refuge* (*ESV*).

Sometimes we think of refuge as hiding out from the storm. But the love of God doesn't just hide you—it *fortifies* you. It becomes your war room. The enemy may still try to speak lies, stir fear, or bring confusion, but when you know the truth of God's love, you rise up and speak *back*.

You say, "No devil, you don't get to define me. You don't get to tell me who I am. I am loved of God, and I am standing in that love today."

And in that love, you find strength to fight, wisdom to discern, and courage to stand.

Earlier in this chapter, we read from Psalm 143:10:

> *Teach me to do your will, for you are my God! Let your good Spirit lead me on level ground* (*ESV*).

That's what His love does. It teaches. It leads. It levels the uneven places in our lives. You may be walking through something that feels unstable right now—something painful or confusing—but I promise you, *God's love is your solid ground.* He's not only walking with you—He's carrying you, surrounding you, and going before you.

Remember when I told you about my sister being in the hospital? She was connected to ventilators, monitors, machines—the works. And I remember looking at all those machines and saying, "You are enemies. You have no authority here." Yes, they were there to help her physically, but spiritually, I could see the assignment of fear and death trying to speak louder than God's promises. And in that moment, I fled to the Lord for refuge—and I stood under the authority of His love.

The love of God doesn't just bring peace—it brings *power.* It gives you boldness to declare the truth over every lie. It anchors you when circumstances try to shake you.

Romans 8:37 says,

> *In all these things we are more than conquerors through him who loved us* (*ESV*).

That verse is such a powerful reminder. It doesn't say we're conquerors because of our strategy or our strength. It says we conquer through Him who loved us. *Love is the weapon.* Love is the victory. Love is the reason you can stand firm and say, "I am not going down. I am going through."

And here's the best part—you don't have to beg God for that love. You don't have to perform for it or earn it. He already gave it.

John 3:16 says,

For God so loved the world, that He gave His only Son, that whoever believes in him should not perish but have eternal life (*ESV*).

Everything you need—salvation, healing, provision, authority—*flows from love.* It was love that sent Jesus. Love that conquered death. Love that declared victory on your behalf. And now, that same love stands over your life as a declaration: you are not alone, and you are not defeated.

And I believe this love is stirring something in you even now. Not just a quiet contentment, but a *holy boldness*. A hunger. An aggression—not against people but against complacency. Against lies. Against anything that tries to steal the truth of who you are in Christ.

This love empowers you to say, "I'm not staying stuck. I'm not shrinking back. I'm pressing in. God has more for me—and I want it."

This is what happens when you get a revelation of the love of God: you stop running *from* the enemy, and you start running *toward* your purpose. And every morning becomes a declaration:

"Lord, awaken my heart. Show me Your steadfast love. Teach me Your will. Lead me on level ground. Because I know who I am—I am Yours."

Final Thoughts

When we talk about *staying hungry*, we're not talking about lack—we're talking about pursuit. We're talking about a heart that's tasted and seen that the Lord is good and now says, "I can't live without more of Him."

Spiritual hunger isn't a weakness; it's a strength. It's the evidence that you've encountered a God so good, so faithful, so loving, that nothing else will satisfy. The more you feast on His Word, the more you want. The more you experience His presence, the more you desire. And that hunger keeps you moving forward—closer to Him, deeper in relationship, stronger in faith, and more confident in who you are.

The enemy wants to distract you, shrink your appetite, twist the truth, and convince you that God is distant or holding back. But the love of God tells a better story. His love fills you, teaches you, leads you, protects you—and calls you into bold obedience. And when you walk in that love, you live a life of fruitfulness, authority, and joy. You live with a fire that doesn't burn out because it's fed daily by fellowship with Him.

So, if your heart is stirred right now—if you feel something rising inside that says, "I want more of God"—then you're right where you need to be.

Stay hungry, because God is preparing a feast. He's drawing you deeper. And there is *so much more* to discover.

Call to Action

Today, make the decision to stay hungry—not out of striving but out of intimacy. Feed daily on the Word. Ask God to enlarge your heart and awaken fresh desire for Him. Don't settle for a life of spiritual maintenance when He's called you to a life of passionate pursuit. Let His love redefine your values, reshape your thinking, and refuel your prayer life. Press in with expectation, because the more you seek Him, the more He reveals. And as you obey out of love, your life will overflow with testimonies, boldness, peace, and fruitfulness. Get ready to be satisfied and stirred at the same time. Because when you stay hungry for God, He never stops pouring out more.

Scriptures Referenced

- Ephesians 3:18–19
- Proverbs 4:18
- Genesis 3:1–5
- Romans 5:8
- James 1:17
- John 10:10
- Philippians 3:8
- Philippians 1:9–11
- Psalm 119:32
- Psalm 34:8
- Matthew 5:6
- John 14:15
- Philippians 1:11
- Galatians 5:22–23
- Psalm 119:105
- Psalm 143:8–10
- Romans 8:37
- John 3:16

Chapter Nine

For the Here and Now

God's love is not something we just read about or look forward to experiencing someday in heaven. It is a present, powerful force—real and transformative in our daily lives. It's for the here and now. In this chapter, we will explore how God's consistent, unrelenting love shapes us, calls us to change, and empowers us to live victoriously today. His love is not just a comforting truth—it is a catalyst for radical transformation and ongoing relationship with Him.

God's Love Is Consistent and Daily

Because God's heart and His love for you are constant, they are daily and consistent. And praise God, His love is not like this world's. The world's love is fickle—dependent on performance, mood, or circumstance. But God's love is the anchor for our souls. And it's not just available on special occasions or when we've "earned" it. No, it's available now.

We've been talking about the comparison between God's love and the world's love. And when you get a revelation of that love, it changes you. It's not a message you just hear once and then move on from. It's a continual invitation. A personal encounter. I love that God is so big and so good that He says, "Let Me show you yet again today how good I am."

This isn't about having someone else's perspective of God or living out of a secondhand revelation. It's not about what your pastor said or what your parents taught, even if they were wonderful teachers. No, this is about you and me having our own relationship with the Lord. Not the enemy's view of Him. Not religion's rigid version of Him. But the real, living God who shows us His love anew every day.

And that's why I love what Paul says in Romans 8:

> *For I am persuaded that neither death nor life, nor angels nor principalities nor powers, nor things present nor things to come, nor height nor depth, nor any other created thing, shall be able to separate us from the love of God which is in Christ Jesus our Lord.*
>
> Romans 8:38-39, *NKJV*

Can we just stop and say, "Wow!"? Nothing—absolutely nothing—can separate you from His love. Not your worst day, not your fears, not your mistakes. Not even the things that haven't happened yet. That's how consistent and present His love is.

And what backs that up for me is Lamentations 3. I remember reading it and just thinking, "Lord, You really are faithful every single morning."

Lamentations 3:22-23 says,

The steadfast love of the Lord never ceases; his mercies never come to an end; they are new every morning; great is your faithfulness (ESV).

Transformational Change

Here's something we don't always want to hear—God is calling us to change. But not just for the sake of change. He wants us to grow because He loves us. And His love is far too good, too big, and too full of purpose to leave us as we are.

Sometimes we adopt this mindset of, "Well, this is as good as it gets." Or maybe we say, "It's better than it's ever been, so I'll just settle here." And I get it—sometimes it feels safer to stop stretching. But can I lovingly challenge that? That attitude of settling is dangerous. Because the Holy Spirit is always leading us, always drawing us deeper. And when we decide, "This is as much as I'm willing to grow," we put a lid on what God can do in us.

I had to confront this in my own life. I had grown in the Lord. I had taught others. But there was a point where I realized—I had stopped being as intentional about my own transformation. And the Lord lovingly pointed it out. Then I realized that I don't want to coast. I want to be constantly renewed by His Spirit.

And that's what Romans 12 talks about. Not just a little tweak here and there—but a total transformation.

Romans 12:2 says,

Do not conform to the pattern of this world, but be transformed by the renewing of your mind. Then you will be able to test and approve what God's will is—his good, pleasing and perfect will (*NIV*).

God isn't calling you to fit into a mold. He's calling you to transformation. And not transformation by effort—but by revelation. It's through His Word. Through relationship. Through His love.

And Paul expands on this in 2 Corinthians 3:18,

And we all, with unveiled face, beholding the glory of the Lord, are being transformed into the same image from one degree of glory to another. For this comes from the Lord who is the Spirit (*ESV*).

This is what God's love does—it keeps pulling us forward, unveiling our hearts so we can behold Him more clearly. We're not stuck. We're not limited. We are being changed—from glory to glory.

And that change isn't something to fear. It's a beautiful invitation. If the Spirit of God is in you, then growth is your portion. Not just in the big moments—but in the daily journey. In your thinking. In your relationships. In your decisions. God's love is calling you to rise.

The Power of Testimony

There's something so powerful about watching real transformation unfold. I spent years ministering in a drug rehab center in Russia, and it was one of the most impactful seasons of my life. We didn't just preach at people—we taught them about the love of God. We didn't focus on what they needed to do for God, but who they were because of Him. We taught them about spirit, soul, and body, and who they had become as new creations in Christ.

I watched people come in covered in sores, addicted, broken, and lost—and I saw them walk out healed, whole, and radiant. I'm telling you, after twelve to eighteen months of being immersed in the truth of God's love, they weren't just better—they were completely transformed. I remember sitting in the front row during their graduation ceremonies and bawling my eyes out as these once-hopeless men and women walked across the stage with strength and joy. You could see the glory of God on their faces.

And I remember so clearly—one day the Holy Spirit asked me, "Carrie, can you say you've changed that much in the last twelve months?" And I sat there stunned, wiping my tears, knowing that while I had been teaching and discipling others, I had let myself plateau. That question stirred something deep inside me. It was the Holy Spirit lovingly challenging me: "Are you growing, too?"

Because the power of God's love is not just for the person next to you—it's for *you*. His love transforms. His love changes you from the inside out. And that transformation should be visible.

That's why I love what it says in Revelation 12:11:

> *And they overcame him by the blood of the Lamb and by the word of their testimony, and they did not love their lives to the death (NKJV).*

There's power in your story. Your testimony isn't just evidence of what God has done—it's a declaration of what His love continues to do. When people see your life, they should see the marks of transformation.

And I hold tightly to this promise:

> *And I am sure of this, that he who began a good work in you will bring it to completion at the day of Jesus Christ.*
>
> Philippians 1:6, *NKJV*

That transformation you experienced when you met Jesus—that was just the beginning. He's not done with you. And the beautiful thing is, He doesn't need you to do it in your own strength. His love fuels the process. His love shapes the journey. And His love ensures the outcome.

So, let me ask you: have you changed in the last 12 months? Has His love done something visible in your life? This isn't a question to condemn you. It's an invitation. Because the same power that transformed those young men and women in Russia—it's available to you, right here and now.

That means every single day, you and I can wake up and know that God's love is right there. It's not leftover from yesterday. It's new. It's fresh. His faithfulness is so consistent that He gives us new mercy for every moment.

So many times, we're looking at what's wrong, what needs fixing, or we're wondering if God's upset with us. But God isn't keeping score the way we do. His heart says, "Let Me love you today. Let Me remind you who you are. Let Me walk with you again."

God's love is not a theological concept to be filed away for Sunday mornings. It is the living reality we are invited to walk in today. You are deeply loved, and that love is doing something in you. It's transforming how you see yourself, how you see God, and how you see the world around you.

Don't wait until heaven to know God loves you. Don't wait until everything is perfect. He wants you to know His love here, in your current reality. That's how present and powerful His love is.

Living Surrendered

Let's talk about something we usually try to avoid: change that requires surrender. The kind of surrender that says, "I trust You, Lord—not just with the big picture, but with the small things. With today." That's what it means to be crucified with Christ. And I'll be honest—most of us don't love the idea. We like being in control. We like planning our spiritual growth. But the Holy Spirit invites us into something so much deeper than self-improvement. He invites us into surrender—into letting go of what we think is best so He can show us what *really* is best.

When you truly believe that God loves you, surrender stops being something you dread and becomes something you desire. Because you trust His heart. You trust that whatever He asks you to lay down, He's got something better to give in return.

There's a verse that has challenged me deeply but also anchored my life. It's Galatians 2:20, and it's one of those verses that you can't just quote—you have to live:

> *I have been crucified with Christ; it is no longer I who live, but Christ lives in me; and the* life *which I now live in the flesh I live by faith in the Son of God, who loved me and gave Himself for me* (*NKJV*).

We often stop at the beginning—"*I have been crucified with Christ*"—and think, *That sounds intense*. And it is. But what makes that verse so powerful isn't just the crucifixion part—it's the ending: "*who loved me and gave Himself for me*." That's the key. You can only lay your life down when you *know* how loved you are. When you know that the One asking for surrender already gave everything for you.

Living crucified with Christ means that the life we live in the flesh, we live by faith. Not by our own faith, but by the faith of the Son of God who lives inside of us. That means we don't have to figure it all out. We just have to walk with Him, trust Him, and yield to Him.

And Jesus didn't ask us to do something He didn't do Himself. In Luke 9:23, He laid it out clearly:

> *Then he said to them all: "Whoever wants to be my disciple must deny themselves and take up their cross daily and follow me"* (*NIV*).

Daily. That's the word that gets me. It's not a one-time surrender at the altar or in a moment of emotional worship. It's daily. It's practical. It's choosing to pause when your flesh wants to react. It's asking, "Holy Spirit, what do You want to do right now?"

Surrender isn't about losing—it's about exchanging. You lay down fear, and He gives you peace. You lay down control, and He gives you direction. You lay down shame, and He clothes you in righteousness. It's not easy, but it's worth it. Because the life you're surrendering was never meant to be lived apart from Him anyway.

So, if you feel Him nudging you today, inviting you to lay something down, don't resist. Say yes. Say, "Lord, I trust You. I know You love me. And I want to live the life You died to give me." That is what it means to be crucified with Christ.

The Daily Decisions

One of the most important things I've learned about walking in God's love is this—it shows up in the day-to-day. Not just in the moments of crisis, or the times we're sitting in church, but in how we live our everyday lives. The choices we make. The way we speak. The thoughts we entertain. This is where the love of God is meant to have its greatest impact.

It's easy to think being led by the Spirit is reserved for "big" decisions—like who to marry, what job to take, or where to move. And yes, He cares about all of that. But even more, He wants to be part of your daily decisions. Things like, how do I respond when I'm frustrated? What do I say when I'm misunderstood? Do I choose peace or let anger take over?

Living by the Spirit means pausing and asking, "Holy Spirit, what do You want to do right now?" It means slowing down long enough to lean into His love instead of reacting from our flesh.

That's what walking in love looks like—it's not always flashy, but it's always transformational.

The Bible gives us such a beautiful picture of this kind of life:

> *Trust in the Lord with all your heart and lean not on your own understanding; in all your ways submit to him, and he will make your paths straight.*
>
> Proverbs 3:5–6, *NIV*

That's not just a Sunday verse—it's a daily invitation. Our own understanding is limited. It's shaped by past experiences, emotions, and fears. But God's understanding is rooted in love. It's steady. And when we trust Him, even when we don't fully understand, He directs our path with clarity.

And I love what Romans 8:14 tells us:

> *For those who are led by the Spirit of God are the children of God* (*NIV*).

Being led by the Spirit isn't about being super-spiritual—it's about being a child. It's about trusting your Father enough to say, "I don't have to have all the answers. I'll go where You lead."

So, what does that look like practically? It might mean choosing gentleness in a tense conversation. It might mean not sending that text you typed in frustration. It might mean taking a moment to breathe and say, "Jesus, help me respond in love."

And let me tell you—when you do that, people notice. They notice that you're different. Not perfect. But peaceful. Anchored.

Steady. That's what the love of God does. It transforms your daily decisions into holy moments of surrender.

Released from Shame and Legalism

One of the greatest lies the enemy tries to sell us is that we have to earn God's love. That somehow, if we just do enough—serve more, pray longer, give bigger—we'll finally qualify. And yet, so many believers live bound by a to-do list, as if righteousness is something we achieve instead of something we receive.

But when you know God loves you—not just in theory, but in your bones—you stop striving. You stop trying to fix yourself so that you're lovable. You stop comparing your spiritual walk to someone else's, because His love isn't measured by performance.

I've met people all over the world who've come to me after teaching on the love of God and said, "How could God love someone like me?" And my response is always the same: "Because He does. He always has. He gave Himself for you." And that love is what sets you free.

Paul talks about this in Philippians 3:8-9. It's one of my favorite passages because it captures the heart of transformation—not by works, but by faith:

> *But more than that, I count everything as loss compared to the priceless privilege* and *supreme advantage of knowing Christ Jesus my Lord ... and may be found in Him ... not having any righteousness of my own derived from [my*

> *obedience to] the Law* and *its rituals, but [possessing] that [genuine righteousness] which comes through faith in Christ* (*AMP*).

That verse changed how I saw myself. I realized I didn't have to live my life trying to be righteous enough for God. I already had His righteousness—because of Jesus. And once you get that, shame starts to fall off. You no longer carry the burden of trying to make yourself worthy. You simply receive what Jesus already paid for.

And when we mess up—and we all do—there's grace for that too. It's not a grace that excuses sin but a grace that forgives and restores.

First John 1:9 says,

> *If we confess our sins, He is faithful and just to forgive us* our *sins and to cleanse us from all unrighteousness* (*NKJV*).

That's the power of the cross. Not just to wipe away your sin but to cleanse you from the residue of it. To remove the shame and guilt that the enemy tries to use to keep you stuck. God doesn't hold your mistakes over your head. He's not keeping a record of your wrongs. He says, "Come to Me. Let Me cleanse you. Let Me remind you who you are."

You are not defined by what you've done. You are defined by who you belong to. And when you truly know His love, you'll find the freedom to live in that identity—confident, whole, and unashamed. Not someday. Not when you've cleaned yourself up, but right here and now.

Experiencing God's Nature

When you know you are loved by God—really know it—you begin to see everything else about Him through that lens. You stop questioning His goodness, His motives, or whether He'll come through for you. Instead, you begin to recognize that every part of who He is flows out of His love. His love isn't just a feeling—it's the foundation of everything He does and everything He is.

This is why 1 John 4:8 speaks so clearly to us:

Whoever does not love does not know God, because God is love (*NIV*).

God doesn't just have love. He *is* love. That means when we talk about who God is—whether He's our healer, our provider, or our peace—we're talking about the expressions of His love. Every name He carries flows from that truth.

When you believe God loves you, you can begin to receive everything else He has for you. That's when Jehovah Rapha isn't just a name—it becomes personal. You begin to say, "You are my healer because You love me."

Exodus 15:26 says,

He said, "...I am the Lord, who heals you" (*NIV*).

Healing isn't earned. It's not a reward. It's a manifestation of His nature. And the same goes for His provision. When you believe He's Jehovah Jireh, it means you trust that the same love that forgives you also provides for you.

Genesis 22:14 says,

So Abraham called that place The LORD Will Provide. And to this day it is said, "On the mountain of the Lord it will be provided" (*NIV*).

And then there's Jehovah Shalom—the Lord is peace. Not just the absence of conflict, but the presence of wholeness. Real peace doesn't come from circumstances—it comes from knowing you're held in the arms of perfect love.

Judges 6:24 says,

So Gideon built an altar to the LORD there and called it The LORD Is Peace (*NIV*).

These names aren't just titles—they are promises. Promises for the here and now. But if you don't know God loves you, you'll hesitate to receive. You'll believe those things are for someone else, someone more qualified, someone with less baggage. But when you know you're loved, you stop striving and start receiving.

You say, "Lord, I receive You as my Healer, my Provider, my Peace—not because I earned it, but because You are love, and You gave Yourself for me."

And when you open your heart like that, the wonders of His nature begin to unfold in your life—not just in theory, but in experience. You begin to see that everything He is, He is for you.

Living in Resurrection Power

God's love didn't just send Jesus to the cross—it raised Him from the dead. And that same resurrection power lives inside of you and me right now. This isn't just a theological idea we nod our heads at in church. It's real. It's active. It's personal.

Sometimes we limit resurrection power to Easter sermons or the moment of salvation. But I want to challenge that. That power is working in you today. It's working in your thoughts, your emotions, your body, and your relationships. It's not waiting for heaven. It's not reserved for spiritual emergencies. It's alive in every part of your everyday life.

Paul said this in Philippians 3, and it stirs something deep in my heart every time I read it:

> *that I may know Him [experientially, becoming more thoroughly acquainted with Him] ... and [in that same way experience] the power of His resurrection*
>
> Philippians 3:10–11, *AMP*

What a powerful statement. Paul didn't just want to know about Jesus—he wanted to know Him. To experience Him. And not just any part of Him, but the *power* of His resurrection. That's the power that brings dead things to life. The kind of power that says, "This doesn't have to stay broken. It doesn't have to stay buried."

I've seen that power at work in countless lives. People healed from disease. Minds restored from trauma. Hearts mended after deep betrayal. That power is real. And it's not far off. It's the Spirit of God, the One who raised Jesus from the dead, and that same Spirit lives in you.

Romans 8:11 says,

And if the Spirit of him who raised Jesus from the dead is living in you, he who raised Christ from the dead will also give life to your mortal bodies because of his Spirit who lives in you (*NIV*).

Did you hear that? Life to your *mortal* body. Not just your spirit. Not just your eternity. Your body. Your life. Your situation. The resurrection isn't just something Jesus did. It's something He gives. It's His ongoing gift of love and power working in us today.

Jesus said it Himself to Martha, right before raising Lazarus from the dead:

Jesus said to her, "I am the resurrection and the life. The one who believes in me will live, even though they die."

John 11:25, *NIV*

He didn't say, "I was" or "I will be." He said, "I *am*." Right now. Living. Present. And powerful. And if He lives in you, then resurrection lives in you too.

So, what feels dead in your life right now? What has the enemy tried to bury? A dream? A relationship? Your sense of worth? I'm here to tell you that resurrection power is not done. Jesus didn't stay in the grave, and neither will the purpose He's placed inside of you.

Speak life. Declare truth. And stand in the confidence that the same power that rolled away the stone is rolling away every lie, every limit, and every label that's tried to keep you bound.

Because of His love, you don't just get to survive—you get to live. And not just someday. Not just when things get better. You get to live in resurrection power—right now.

Final Thoughts

The love of God is not just a message—it's a movement in your life. It's daily, consistent, empowering, and present. It doesn't wait for heaven to start its work. It transforms you right now. In every area—your mindset, your habits, your relationships—His love is actively at work.

Don't settle for "better than before." Don't settle for "as good as it gets." Let His love pull you deeper, lift you higher, and empower you to live fully in the here and now.

Call to Action

Ask the Lord to show you where you've settled. Invite Him into the places where you've accepted limitation or stopped believing for transformation. Surrender control—not just once, but daily. Let His love lead. Let His Spirit guide your choices. And allow the resurrection power of Jesus to fill your today with boldness, peace, purpose, and joy. Stop hiding. Stop doubting. The world needs what God has placed in you. You were made for such a time as this.

Scriptures Referenced

- Romans 8:38–39
- Lamentations 3:22–23
- Romans 12:2
- 2 Corinthians 3:18
- Revelation 12:11
- Philippians 1:6
- Galatians 2:20
- Luke 9:23
- Proverbs 3:5–6
- Romans 8:14
- Philippians 3:8–9
- 1 John 1:9
- 1 John 4:8
- Exodus 15:26
- Genesis 22:14
- Judges 6:24
- Philippians 3:10–11
- Romans 8:11
- John 11:25

Chapter Ten

Created to Flourish

I've known the Lord since I was six years old. So, for a long time now, I've been walking with Him, growing in this relationship, and one thing I can say with absolute certainty is this—God is faithful to complete that which He started. The work He began in you isn't over, and it certainly isn't small. It's a flourishing, growing, bursting-forth kind of work, because that's the nature of His love. His love never does anything halfway.

This chapter is about recognizing that you weren't just saved to survive—you were created to flourish. And not just at the very end of your life when you stand before the Lord, but right now, in every area of your life: your marriage, your kids, your finances, your dreams, your purpose, your identity. God's not just waiting to complete His work someday—He's doing it now. You were created for abundance, not lack. Expansion, not limitation. Overflow, not fear.

And I want to encourage you with this: the hunger you feel for more is the Holy Spirit stirring within you. That longing for testimony in your life, for healing, for peace, for provision—it's not wishful thinking. It's the Spirit of God saying, "I have something more for you."

As we go through this chapter, we're going to look at the good work God is doing inside of you and how His Word reveals what that flourishing life looks like. We're going to unpack how the promises of God, which are rooted in His nature, invite you to participate in the divine nature, not just visit it occasionally. And most importantly, we're going to settle it once and for all—you are loved, and because of that love, you were created to flourish.

God's Faithfulness to Complete His Work

There's something so powerful about knowing—not just hoping or wondering—but truly knowing that God finishes what He starts. Philippians 1:6 says it best:

> *And I am sure of this, that he who began a good work in you will bring it to completion at the day of Jesus Christ* (*ESV*).

I love how it says, "*I am sure of this.*" There's no hesitation, no question mark, no if. Paul didn't write that from a place of uncertainty—he wrote it from conviction. And that's the same conviction I want to stir in your heart today. You can be sure of this: God is not done with you.

We often read that verse and think, "Well, okay, one day—maybe when I'm standing before the Lord in eternity—then this work will be finished." And while yes, the full picture comes into focus when we see Him face to face, that doesn't mean the rest of your life is meant to be lived in spiritual neutral until that moment. No, the truth is that there is a continual good work happening right now.

You didn't just get saved and then placed on a shelf to wait. Praise God! No, the moment you received salvation, God began a work in you—a work that is meant to flourish, expand, abound, and bear fruit. And I want to tell you today, there is momentum in the Spirit. There is movement in your life. You may not feel it every day, but God's love is actively producing something within you. You were created for more than just holding onto faith until heaven. You were created to flourish in the here and now.

I remember digging into the word "*good*" from this verse, and what I found stirred something deep in me. It's not just referring to a morally good or ethically right work. No, the meaning of "good" here is much richer. It means to flourish, to expand, to lavish, to burst forth, to excel, to abound, to increase—this is the nature of the work God is doing inside of you. Not small. Not basic. Not just functional. It's extravagant!

So, when Paul says, "*he who began a good work,*" he's saying, "he who began this flourishing, expanding, bursting-forth work in you." That changes how you look at your journey, doesn't it?

I don't know about you, but I have this deep hunger to see just how much God can do in my life. I want my marriage to thrive, not just survive. I want to walk in testimonies that I can pass on to my children—not just stories from the past, but miracles unfolding in our home right now. I told Mike once, "I believe our house is going to be paid off in two years." And he looked at me and said, "Really?" And I said, "Yeah." Why? Because I'm hungry to see the goodness of God—not someday, but now. I desire to see signs, wonders, and miracles. And I know I'm not the only one.

If you're reading this and something is stirring in your spirit—a desire, a hope, a longing for more—then I want to tell you, that's not just you. That's the Holy Spirit within you bearing witness. He's saying, "Yes. That good work? That flourishing, bursting-out, kingdom-advancing work? That's what I'm doing in you."

And maybe you've had some hiccups in your journey. Maybe there have been seasons of wandering, or times when it felt like everything stalled out. I get that. But let me tell you—God is still faithful. He hasn't forgotten you. He hasn't changed His mind about you. The work He started, He will complete. Not maybe. Not if. He will.

So, let's agree with that today. Let's take hold of that promise and declare it, not with doubt, but with boldness:

"He who began a good work in me will bring it to completion."

That's your promise. And you were created to flourish in the fullness of it.

The Nature of a "Good Work"

When we read that God began a *good* work in us, we often gloss over that word "good," don't we? We think it simply means "nice" or "not bad"—but the Word of God doesn't use casual language. The Holy Spirit is intentional, and that one word—*good*—is loaded with power. And if we don't understand the nature of what that *good work* is, we can settle for far less than what God actually intended for our lives.

As I continued to study this passage, I asked myself: What does the word "good" really mean? Is it just referring to getting saved? Is it just talking about stopping destructive behaviors? Yes, those are all part of it—salvation, healing from addiction, freedom from lies and depression—those are absolutely good. But the original meaning goes even deeper.

The definitions I found were amazing. As I mentioned previously, the word "good" in this context means to flourish, to expand, to lavish, to burst forth, to burst out, to increase, to excel. It even implies beauty, excellence, and abundance. Isn't that just like our God?

God didn't begin a "*barely-make-it*" work in you. He didn't start a work that would just manage to hold your life together until you get to heaven. No, He began a flourishing, thriving, growing, ever-increasing work in you, one that is meant to impact not just your eternity but your everyday. That's the nature of a good work. It's not just about spiritual survival—it's about supernatural fruitfulness.

Let me ask you something: Are you hungry to see what God can do in your life? I know I am. I want to see how far His goodness can stretch in my marriage, in my family, in my finances, in my purpose. That hunger is from Him. He placed it there because He knows what He deposited in you. He wants you to dream with Him. He wants you to believe for flourishing—not in your own strength, but because of what He has already started inside of you.

And here's the thing: You don't have to manufacture this growth. You don't have to try harder, strive more, or hustle to make it happen. God is the One who started the good work. And

He's the One who will bring it to completion. Your job is simply to believe what He's said about you—to look into His Word and say, "Yes, Lord, that's who I am."

You were never meant to just tread water. You were never meant to live in spiritual poverty, stuck in the same cycles, looking at everyone else's life and wondering why they're so blessed. No, you were created to flourish. And not just in theory—in truth, in your real, everyday life.

So, if you've been living small, thinking small, expecting small—I want to shake that off of you today. Because when the Spirit of God lives inside of you, you carry His nature. And His nature is to flourish. His nature is to expand and increase. His nature is to overflow with goodness and grace and power and provision. That's the "good work" He's doing in you.

You might not feel like it right now. Maybe life feels a little dry, maybe even barren. But friend, can I remind you that seeds don't shout when they grow? But they are growing. Quietly. Powerfully. Steadily. And one day, there's going to be fruit that testifies—God was at work all along.

Don't minimize the work of God in you. Don't call it small when He calls it flourishing. Agree with Him. Declare it with boldness. And believe that His version of "good" is so much more than you ever imagined.

"He who began a flourishing, expanding, abounding, bursting-forth work in you will bring it to completion." That is your promise. That is your reality. And that is the nature of the good work within you.

Hunger and Expectation for More

There's a difference between discontentment and holy hunger. One comes from dissatisfaction; the other comes from revelation. Discontentment will wear you out, but holy hunger will stir you up. It's not about being unhappy with what you have—it's about knowing there's more of God to experience, and you were designed to crave it.

I believe that kind of hunger—the kind that expects more from God—isn't just some spiritual ambition. It's actually a sign of intimacy. It's a sign that you're listening to the Spirit of God. When you start feeling that pull to believe for greater things, that desire to see His hand move in fresh ways in your life—it's not arrogance, and it's not foolishness. It's the Spirit of God inside of you saying, "I have more. Will you believe Me for it?"

You see, when you understand the nature of God's love, you stop putting limits on what He can do. You begin to approach Him not as someone you're trying to convince to bless you, but as a Father who's already decided to bless you abundantly. That's when your expectations start to rise—not based on your performance but based on His promises.

For many years, I looked at the promises of God like they were future goals—things that might one day happen if I just stayed faithful enough, worked hard enough, and matured spiritually. I'd underline verses in my Bible, highlight them, stick Post-it notes all over the pages, and write "someday." But as I grew in the revelation of God's love, I realized those promises weren't just for a more spiritual version of me down the road—they were for me right now. Today. Because I am loved by God today.

And you are too. That hunger you feel, that longing to see your kids flourish in their callings, to experience supernatural healing in your body, to walk in provision, peace, and boldness, that's not just wishful thinking. That's evidence. Evidence of the Spirit of God working within you, reminding you that you were created for more than what you've currently seen.

That hunger leads you to declare things in faith that challenge your current circumstances. Things like:

"Lord, I believe this sickness has no authority in my body."
"God, I know you have a calling for me that hasn't even been revealed yet."
"Father, I believe You are restoring joy in my marriage and peace in my home."
"Jesus, I trust You with my children's future—I don't need to live in fear of this world."

These are the words of someone who's learning to listen to the voice of love—not the voice of fear. Because fear will always lower the ceiling on your expectations. Fear will tell you to scale back, to play it safe, to manage your hope. But love invites you to dream again. To believe again. To step out again.

You may have had disappointments. You may even feel like your faith has been bruised. But God isn't afraid of your big prayers. In fact, He delights in them. He's not watching your life from a distance, hoping you don't ask for too much. He's the One stirring your heart to ask for more.

Ephesians 3:20 says,

Now to Him who is able to do exceedingly abundantly above all that we ask or think, according to the power that works in us (*NKJV*).

That's the nature of the God who lives inside of you. Exceedingly. Abundantly. Above. That's not a motivational phrase—it's a kingdom reality. When you anchor yourself in His love, that reality becomes yours.

And here's what I want you to hear today: your hunger is not a flaw. It's not a sign that you're ungrateful or unspiritual. It's a sign that you know there's more, and you're refusing to settle for anything less than the full inheritance Jesus died to give you.

So let that hunger grow. Let that holy expectation rise up in you. Let your prayers be bold, your declarations be firm, and your heart be full of anticipation—not because you're trying to force something to happen, but because you know who your Father is.

You were not created to settle.
You were not created to shrink back.
You were created to flourish.

That flourishing starts with hunger—and it grows through expectation. Say it with confidence: "Lord, I'm ready. Stir my faith. Lead me into more. I trust You to fulfill every promise, because I know You love me."

No Room for Fear

One of the greatest revelations that will absolutely destroy fear in your life is this: God is for you.

Not maybe. Not sometimes. Not only when you've done everything right. He is for you. Period.

Romans 8:30–31 says,

> *Moreover, whom He predestined, these He also called; whom He called, these He also justified; and whom He justified, these He also glorified. What then shall we say to these things? If God is for us, who* can be *against us?* (*NKJV*).

Now here's what I want to point out—we often read that last part as a question, right? Like, "*If God is for us…? Who can be against us…?*" And then we start to quietly list all the possibilities: Well, sickness could be against me… debt could be against me… inflation… fear for my kids… the world going crazy… trauma from my past… That little voice of fear starts putting question marks where God put exclamation points.

But that's not how Paul meant it. He wasn't asking a question—he was declaring a truth. This is a victory statement. A war cry. A bold, defiant, Spirit-filled declaration against anything that dares oppose you as a child of God.

If God is for me—*nothing* can be against me!

Not sickness.
Not fear.
Not poverty.
Not generational trauma.
Not shame.
Not failure.
Not even death.

Because the preceding verse says—He called you, He justified you, and He has already glorified you. You are not in some holding pattern of "maybe" with God. You are His. You've been chosen, declared righteous, and stamped with glory—His glory, not yours.

And that's what gives you authority. That's what stirs up the kind of boldness that makes the enemy nervous. When you know God is for you, fear loses its place in your life.

See, fear thrives where love is questioned. Fear gets loud when we're unsure of where we stand. But when you know that God is not only with you—but *for* you, working on your behalf, rooting for your success, empowering your every step—fear has no room to speak.

You stop saying things like:
"I hope God comes through for me this time."
"I just don't know if I'm strong enough."
"I guess this is just the way life is."
And instead, you start declaring: "God is for me—so nothing can succeed against me."
"God is for my marriage, so restoration is mine."
"God is for my healing, so I will walk in divine health."
"God is for my children, so I refuse to fear for their future."
"God has a future and purpose for my life."

This isn't blind optimism—this is grounded in the unshakable reality of God's love and Word. That's what Paul is shouting in Romans. He's saying: look at all the things God has already done—called, justified, glorified—and then try to tell me there's something that could stand against me! There's not.

But here's the catch—you have to agree with it. No one can believe it for you. I can say it over your life until I'm blue in the face: "You're loved. You're chosen. You're victorious." But until you say Amen to that truth, it won't transform you. You're the one who has to say it. Out loud. From the heart.

Because agreement is powerful. It aligns your words with heaven's declaration. And when you know your God—when you know His heart, His love, His faithfulness—then "*If God is for me!*" becomes a settled, unshakable conviction in your spirit.

Not a question. Not a maybe. A bold, fearless declaration.

So, I want to ask you: What would your life look like if you really believed that God was for you? What would change in your thoughts, your prayers, your choices? How would you talk to fear if you believed heaven had your back?

I'll tell you what would happen—you'd get an attitude. And not just any attitude—a boldness rooted in love. The kind of attitude that makes you look at the devil and say, "Who do you think you are, touching my kids, messing with my finances, whispering lies in my head? I am loved of God. And that means I am not afraid of you."

That kind of love-filled boldness doesn't come from wishful thinking. It comes from revelation. From knowing your God. From looking into His Word and seeing your reflection in His promises. From waking up every morning, not with dread, but with this conviction: If God is for me—who can be against me?

No one.
Nothing.
No fear.

No failure.
No future threat.

God is for you. And that changes everything.

God's Divine Provision for Life and Godliness

One of the greatest lies the enemy wants you to believe is that you're limited by where you came from—your family background, your education, your past mistakes, your current situation. That somehow, what you've experienced or what you lack disqualifies you from walking in the fullness of God's promises.

But I want to tell you something that will absolutely shatter that lie:

> *His divine power has granted to us all things that pertain to life and godliness, through the knowledge of him who called us to his own glory and excellence.*
>
> 2 Peter 1:3, *ESV*

Did you catch that? All things. Not some. Not a few things, depending on your performance. All things. Everything you need for this life and to walk in godliness has already been granted to you—by His divine power, not your human effort. That means you are not waiting for God to finally provide. He already has. It's done. It's been granted.

And I love how it says, "*through the knowledge of him.*" You begin to walk in these things as you grow in the knowledge of who God is. Because when you understand who He is—His love,

His nature, His promises—you realize just how much has already been made available to you. God doesn't give based on who we are. He gives based on who He is.

The verse says He called us to His own glory and excellence. He didn't look at us and say, "Wow, you're really holy and excellent, so I'm going to grant you everything." No—He looked at us through His love and said, "Because I am glorious, because I am excellent, I'm calling you into that same glory. I'm inviting you into a life that reflects My nature."

That's the kind of invitation that turns your whole life upside down in the best way. You begin to realize: I'm not limited by my story. I'm not bound by where I grew up or what I didn't have. I'm not chained to fear, shame, debt, lack, or confusion. God has already granted me everything I need.

But the world—and even religion—will try to convince you otherwise. "Well, if you want God's provision, you'd better work for it." "If you want peace, you need to earn it." "If you want to be used by God, you need to prove yourself."

But here's the truth: Jesus already did the proving. And because of Him, you've been given access to a life that overflows with power, peace, and purpose. This provision isn't earned—it's inherited. And the enemy hates that.

That's why he tries to distract you with comparisons: "Look at her life—she was born into privilege. Of course, she's flourishing," or "He's got connections and open doors—I'll never have that." Comparison is a tactic straight from hell. Because it gets your eyes off of God's provision and onto your own lack. If you're constantly measuring what you think you have against what others seem to have, you'll miss what's been *granted* to you.

Let me say this loud and clear: The narrative of the world is not your final story. Your past is not your blueprint. Your circumstances are not your ceiling. What God has provided in Christ is your truth, your inheritance, your present reality. You have been given everything—*everything*—you need for life and godliness.

And listen, this isn't just "churchy" language. This is real-life truth. That means you have what you need for your marriage, your parenting, your business, your health, your relationships. Everything that pertains to life and to walking in the character and power of God—it's already in your spiritual account. You are not spiritually broke. You are fully funded by Heaven.

That doesn't mean life will always be easy, but it does mean you are never without the resources of God to walk through it. And the more you know Him—really know Him—the more confident you become in accessing what's yours.

So, I want to ask you—where have you been saying, "I just don't have what it takes"? What areas have you labeled as impossible, unreachable, or too far gone? Wherever those places are, I want you to lay 2 Peter 1:3 right on top of them like a banner. Let it speak louder than your doubts:

"His divine power has granted to me all things that pertain to life and godliness."

Start saying it out loud. Start declaring it over your day, over your finances, over your children, over your ministry. Not because you're trying to convince God to do something—but because you're aligning with what He's already done.

You're not stuck. You're not lacking. You're not disqualified. You're equipped. You're empowered. And you are provided for. Because God is not just good—He is generous.

The Power of God's Promises

We live in a world full of broken promises. People promise you the world, but then walk away. Circumstances promise security, and then things shift. Even our own emotions make promises—"If I just get that one thing, I'll be happy"—only to leave us empty. But when God makes a promise, it's different. It's holy. It's solid. And it's powerful—because it comes from His nature.

Second Peter 1:4 says,

> *By which he has granted to us his precious and very great promises, so that through them you may become partakers of the divine nature, having escaped from the corruption that is in the world because of sinful desire* (*ESV*).

Let that settle in for a moment. His precious and very great promises. I love that it doesn't just say "promises." It doesn't even just say "great promises." It says precious—which means treasured, valuable, deeply cherished by God—and very great—which means massive, abundant, surpassing anything this world could offer.

Why are they precious? Because they are tied directly to the nature of God. They're not random words on paper. They are divine guarantees breathed out by the Spirit of God. Every promise you read in the Word—whether it's about healing, provision, peace, protection, righteousness, purpose—it all comes from who He is. That's why you can trust it. Because God cannot lie, and He never separates what He says from who He is.

That's why when we talk about God's promises, we're not talking about wishes. We're not talking about vague hopes. We're talking about real, legal inheritance granted to you by your Father. You are not begging for scraps. You are partaking of divine provision.

And look at what the verse says: "*So that through them you may become partakers of the divine nature.*" That's not poetic—it's literal. Through the promises of God, you're not just receiving a blessing—you're participating in the very nature of God Himself.

Do you need healing? That's not just a prayer request—that's a manifestation of Jehovah Rapha, the Lord your Healer. Do you need peace? You're not just trying to calm down—you are walking with the Prince of Peace. Do you need provision? Jehovah Jireh, the Lord your Provider, is your Source. Do you feel broken? El Shaddai, the All-Sufficient One, lives in you.

These are not just promises—they're expressions of who God is, and they've been granted to you.

And that word "granted"—it's past tense. It means it's already yours. Not "will be yours someday if you do enough." It's already been given. That changes how you pray. That changes how you face fear. That changes how you read the Bible. You stop striving for what's already been handed to you and start believing and receiving.

Let me encourage you with something I often share with our students at Charis: you cannot separate your relationship with God from your relationship with the Word of God because His promises reveal His heart. His promises reveal what He wants for you, how He sees you, and what He has made available to you. And when you begin to read the Word, not through a lens of religion or obligation, but through the lens of love, you'll start to say, "Wait a second—this belongs to me!"

When you see it that way, you stop quoting Scripture out of desperation, and you start speaking it with conviction. You don't just say, "God will supply all my needs," as a wish. You say it with boldness: "God, You love me. And because You love me, I believe every promise You made is true for me. You've supplied everything I need."

There's a big difference between *repeating* a verse to try to convince yourself and *declaring* it because you believe it's your inheritance. And that belief is anchored in one thing: knowing you are loved.

When you see the promises of God as an extension of His love, they become unshakable to you. They're not dependent on your performance. They're based on His perfection. That's what makes them powerful.

So, when the enemy whispers, "Well, maybe that healing isn't for you," you respond with, "Actually, it is, because the promise was made, and it was made out of love." When doubt creeps in and says, "What if your children never come back to the Lord?", you declare, "No, the promises of God say they will, and I'm partaking in His divine nature—so I don't have to live in fear."

Friend, the promises of God are your weapons. They're your inheritance. They're your daily bread. And when you open the Word and find one, I want you to hold it close. Speak it. Believe it. Declare it. Not because it sounds good, but because it came from a Father who loves you and has already declared, "This is yours."

God's promises aren't distant—they're personal.
They're not just poetic—they're powerful.
And they don't just describe blessings—they invite you into God's very nature.

So go ahead. Believe big. Expect much. Because you are loved deeply. And every promise is proof.

Truth vs. Facts – The Higher Reality

One of the most freeing revelations you can ever receive is this: there's a difference between facts and truth. And that difference is everything.

See, facts may tell you what's happening in the natural, but truth declares what is unchanging in the Spirit. Facts are subject to change. Truth never is.

You might be facing very real situations. You might say, "Carrie, it's a fact—I'm sick. It's a fact—my bank account is empty. It's a fact—my marriage is hanging by a thread. It's a fact—I haven't heard from my children in years." And I won't argue with you. I won't deny the pain or the difficulty. But here's what I will say to you: those facts don't get the final word.

God's truth is greater than every fact. Not just marginally greater—completely able to transform every fact into a testimony of His goodness. His truth overrides the facts because it comes from His unshakable love and eternal nature.

And let me be clear: acknowledging truth doesn't mean pretending the facts aren't real. It means declaring that there's a greater reality that has the authority to change the situation. You're not ignoring what you see—you're choosing to put your confidence in what God says above what you see.

Let me give you an example straight from the heart: maybe it's a fact that your child has wandered away from God. That's heartbreaking. It's a fact that you haven't heard from them in a long time. And maybe every time the phone rings, your heart jumps, hoping it's them. That's a real emotion. But truth says this—God knows exactly where they are. He knows who to send across their path. He knows how to reach their heart in a way that you never could. That's the higher reality.

And when you begin to speak truth over that situation—"Lord, You love my child more than I do. You are bringing godly influences around them. You are speaking to their heart. Your goodness is chasing them down"—you move from anxiety to peace. You hand them over to God's love. And friend, that's the safest place they could ever be.

Or maybe it's a fact that the doctor gave you a report that shook you. Maybe your body is feeling the symptoms. But here's what truth says:

"By His stripes, you were healed."
"The same Spirit that raised Christ from the dead lives in you."
"He sent His Word and healed them."

When you hold those truths up to the facts, you're not denying the diagnosis—you're confronting it with a higher authority.

We've got to stop thinking that truth and facts are the same thing. There aren't "old truths" and "new truths." There is truth—and there are lies. And the enemy will use every lie he can to make your facts look permanent. But he's a deceiver. And his voice often comes in the first person, doesn't it?

"I'm never going to get better."
"I'm always going to be broke."
"I'll never be good enough for God to use me."

That's not you talking. That's the devil trying to impersonate your voice, so you'll own the lie. But you need to stop mid-thought and say, "Wait a minute. That's not the real me. That's not the truth. The truth is—I am healed. I am chosen. I am called. I am equipped. I am loved."

And you don't speak those truths to try to convince yourself. You speak them with the conviction of someone who knows who their Father is. You speak them because the Word of God—not your feelings, not your symptoms, not your bank account—is your anchor.

When you speak truth like that—anchored in the love of God—it becomes a sword in your hand, not just a bandage for your wounds.

So, let me ask you: what facts have you been agreeing with lately? What lies have slipped in under the radar, disguising themselves as "just the way it is"? Because today is the day you draw a line and say, "No more. I will not define my life by the facts. I will define it by the truth of God's Word."

And here's what the truth says:
You are more than a conqueror.
You are filled with the fullness of God.
You are the righteousness of God in Christ.
You have everything you need for life and godliness.
You are flourishing.
You are healed.
You are whole.
You are loved.

Let the truth speak louder than the facts.

You weren't created to live under circumstances—you were created to rise above them.
You weren't created to manage fear—you were created to overcome by faith.
And that faith works by love.
And love speaks the truth.

So, speak it. Declare it. Believe it. Truth is the higher reality. And truth sets you free.

The Mirror of the Word

We all look in the mirror every day. For most of us, it's the first thing we do when we wake up—checking to see what needs to be fixed, what's out of place, what changed overnight. But have you ever noticed that when you look into a mirror, you're rarely looking to see what's *right*? More often than not, we're looking for the flaws. We're trained by the world—and by our own insecurity—to focus on what's lacking.

But God gives us a different kind of mirror. It's called the Word. And unlike the natural mirror that reflects your physical appearance, this spiritual mirror reveals your true identity—who you are in Christ right now, not who you used to be or who you hope to become someday.

James 1:22–25 says it this way:

> *But be doers of the word, and not hearers only, deceiving yourselves. For if anyone is a hearer of the word and not a doer, he is like a man who looks intently at his natural face in a mirror. For he looks at himself and goes away and at once forgets what he was like. But the one who looks into the perfect law, the law of liberty, and perseveres, being no hearer who forgets but a doer who acts, he will be blessed in his doing* (ESV).

That phrase "perfect law of liberty"—oh, I love that. It means this Word doesn't bind you—it frees you. This mirror isn't reminding you of how far you have to go. It's revealing what God has already accomplished in you through Christ. It shows you what has been completed. It's not projecting who you *might* be in ten years if you work hard enough. It's saying, "This is who you are now."

When I was younger, I used to read the Bible with all my highlighters and pens and sticky notes—underlining verses with this mindset: *Someday, when I'm more spiritual... Someday, when I've figured it all out... Someday, when I'm worthy, I'll walk in these things*. I didn't realize that the Word wasn't a set of future goals—it was a present revelation.

It's not a mirror to show you what's wrong with you. It's a mirror to show you who you already are in Christ. And when you look into it—and I mean really look—you're not supposed to walk away and forget what you saw. But that's what happens when we only hear the Word and don't do it. James says we deceive ourselves. Not because God's Word doesn't work, but because we've forgotten what it said about us.

This is why the enemy fights so hard to keep you from the Word. Because he knows if you look into this mirror long enough, you'll stop believing the lies he's been whispering. You'll stop identifying with the old you and start walking in the confidence of the new you. The healed you. The free you. The anointed you. The loved-by-God you.

And let me tell you something: the devil isn't scared of you reading your Bible—he's terrified of you believing what it says. That's the difference between being a hearer and a doer. A hearer gathers information. A doer walks in transformation.

So how do you keep from forgetting? You go back to the mirror. Again, and again, and again. Not to fix something, but to remember who you are. Because this world is constantly trying to paint a different picture of you. It's trying to create a new identity for you based on your past, your performance, or your pain. But the Word doesn't operate like that. The Word reminds you:

"You are chosen."
"You are holy."
"You are a new creation."

"You are righteous."

"You are seated in heavenly places with Christ."

This is your reality. This is your reflection. And the more you look into this perfect law of liberty, the more you begin to act like who you really are.

I always tell people: don't read the Bible like it's a checklist or a report card. Read it like it's a love letter and a mirror. Every promise, every truth, every instruction—it's showing you your real face. And when you persevere in it—when you refuse to let go of what it says about you—you'll start to see those truths become your daily experience.

You'll go from defeated to victorious. From confused to confident. From striving to resting. From fear to boldness. All because you chose to believe what the mirror said.

So go ahead—open the Word, look into it deeply, and don't walk away forgetting. Walk away transformed. Because this mirror doesn't lie. It reveals. It liberates. It blesses. And most of all—it reminds you that you were created to flourish.

Authority and Identity

If the enemy can convince you that you're unloved, he can rob you of your authority. But when you're rooted in love—when you *know* you're loved—you start to rise up differently. You stop tolerating lies, sickness, lack, fear, and defeat. You stop begging and start declaring. Why? Because now you're standing in your true identity. And that identity is backed by the power of heaven.

Love isn't just a warm feeling from God—it's the foundation of your authority. That's why Galatians 5:6 says that faith works through love. When you understand the love of God, your faith takes on a whole new confidence. It's not timid. It's not unsure. It's bold. And that's the kind of faith that moves mountains and makes the devil tremble.

See, many people try to operate in spiritual authority without first knowing who they are. They try to cast out fear, speak to sickness, and resist the enemy—but if they're unsure about their identity, their authority feels weak and shaky. Why? Because authority flows from identity, and identity is grounded in love.

You can't walk in your God-given authority if you think God's disappointed in you. You won't resist the enemy boldly if you're not sure the Father is on your side. But once you get it deep down—I am loved by God—you start to see everything differently. You stop asking, "Am I good enough for God to use me?" and you start declaring, "Who do you think you are, devil, touching the beloved of the Lord?"

Let me tell you how this plays out in real life—because I'm not just talking about big theological ideas. I'm talking about how we teach our own kids to walk in this truth.

There was a moment with my son Michael that I'll never forget. He was having a hard time and started saying things like, "I'm just a dummy... I'm such a loser... I'm so stupid." And my heart just stopped. I immediately said, "Whoa, whoa, whoa—hold on, buddy."

I got down at eye level with him and asked, "Who talks like that to you? Does Mom talk like that? Does Dad talk like that?" And with tears in his eyes, he said, "No." And I said, "That's right.

The devil talks like that. And you don't have to let the devil lie to you."

Then I reminded him, "You are loved by God. You are chosen. You are filled with healing. Who does the devil think he is, trying to tell you otherwise?" That moment wasn't just about correcting behavior—it was about reestablishing identity.

You see, this is how we train our kids—not just to behave well, but to understand their authority through God's love. When they come to us with a tummy ache, we don't just say, "Let's pray and hope God heals." No, we say, "You have healing inside of you. The fullness of God lives in you. The healer lives in your body. Who does the devil think he is, trying to put sickness on the beloved of the Lord?"

That's the kind of attitude love produces. That's the kind of authority love awakens.

When you walk into a room and know you're loved, you walk in differently. You pray differently. You parent differently. You speak to circumstances with a confidence that isn't rooted in your performance—but in His affection.

You're not bold because you're strong—you're bold because you're secure.
You're not powerful because you've got it all figured out—you're powerful because you know who your Daddy is.
You're not confident because of who you are—you're confident because of whose you are.

So, if you've been feeling timid in your faith, unsure of your prayers, uncertain about your authority—it's not because you're broken. It's just a sign that your revelation of God's love needs to go deeper. And guess what? That's a beautiful place to be, because God loves to show you how deeply loved you are.

So, ask Him. Say, "Lord, remind me who I am. Remind me who You are. Let me walk in the boldness of being loved." Because the moment that truth hits your spirit, something shifts.

You stop asking for permission to be victorious, and you start enforcing the victory Jesus already won for you. You stop tolerating fear and defeat, and you start walking in power and peace. You stop trying to be worthy of authority—and you start using it.

That's the kind of confidence the enemy can't stand. And that's the kind of life you were created to live.

You were not just created to receive love—you were created to walk in the authority that love empowers. And when you know you're loved, the supernatural becomes your new normal.

Now, Not Later

Another dangerous lie the enemy uses to rob us of the life God has planned for us is the idea that it's *for later*.

Healing? That's coming... someday.
Provision? Eventually, when you've earned it.
Calling and purpose? In the future, once you've matured.
Peace? Maybe one day, when life finally calms down.

But that's not what God's Word says. That's not what His love reveals. God's love is for you now. Not later. Not eventually. Not someday. Now.

And yet, religion so often trains us to delay. It teaches us to look at our spiritual lives like a to-do list we haven't completed yet. "Well, you can't expect God to bless you if you haven't..." You fill in the blank: read enough, prayed enough, repented enough, proved yourself enough. But the whole point of God's love is that it's not about what you do for Him—it's about what He's already done for you.

Galatians 5:6 says it like this:

> *For in Christ Jesus neither circumcision nor uncircumcision counts for anything, but only faith working through love (ESV).*

Not performance. Not rituals. Not spiritual checklists. Only faith. And that faith works through love.

That means your confidence to receive healing, provision, joy, peace, identity—it's not found in what you've done. It's found in knowing that you are deeply, unconditionally loved by God. That love stirs up a boldness inside you. That love births faith. And faith works now—because God's love is present now.

That changed everything.

It means that healing wasn't some goal for the future—it was a present reality. It meant that I didn't need to strive for acceptance—I already had it. It meant that I could declare, "I am whole, I am chosen, I am full of power," not as a wish, but as a truth grounded in love.

And let me just say this—you are not at the back door of the kingdom, peeking in, watching everyone else receive blessings while you're still "working your way up." You're not in the waiting room of spiritual worthiness. You are seated at the table. You are in Christ. And everything He purchased is already yours.

That's why the psalmist prayed this in Psalm 143:8:

Let the morning bring me word of your unfailing love, for I have put my trust in you. Show me the way I should go, for to you I entrust my life (NIV).

Do you hear the urgency in that prayer? The expectation? "*Let the morning bring me word...*" Not next week. Not after I fix myself. Not when I've proven my devotion. Right now. This morning. I want to wake up and know: I am loved. I am guided. I am held by You.

And you know what? That's exactly what God wants too. He wants you waking up in the morning, not wondering where you stand with Him, but fully confident: *I am loved today. I am empowered today. I have everything I need today.*

Let me challenge you—stop underlining promises for the future and start claiming them for the present. Stop looking at healing as a distant hope and start declaring, "Because You love me, I am healed." Stop delaying your joy and start saying, "Because You love me, I can rejoice now." Stop putting off your breakthrough and start declaring, "Because You love me, I am free today."

Every moment you wait to believe God's love is a moment the enemy will try to fill with fear, shame, or doubt. But when you say yes to love now, you step into the truth of your identity now. And that's where transformation happens.

You were created to flourish now. You were created to walk in abundance now. You were created to be whole, free, filled, and empowered—now.

So don't wait. Don't put off what God's already declared. The Word was written for you today. The promises are active today. His presence is here today. And faith is working through love today.

Love isn't a theory. It's not an emotion. It's a Person. And that Person—Jesus—lives in you right now. And that changes everything.

Final Thoughts

You were not created for survival—you were created to flourish. You weren't placed on this earth to simply endure, hoping to make it through life without falling apart. No, you were designed by a loving Father to overflow with His goodness, to walk in wholeness, and to live every day grounded in your identity as a beloved child of God.

Throughout this chapter—and truly throughout this entire book—we've seen that the foundation of the Christian life isn't effort, striving, or performance. It's love. God's love for you is not a vague theological concept—it's a transformational force. It is the power behind your healing, the fuel for your identity, the anchor for your faith, and the catalyst for your authority. His love is the reason every promise is yes and amen.

You don't have to wait until you're "better" to experience all that God has for you. You don't have to grow into it slowly, dragging guilt and shame behind you. God's goodness is for now. His presence is for now. His promises are for now. Why? Because His love is for now. And when you receive that, everything changes.

So, as you close this final chapter, I want you to see your life not through the lens of your past or your limitations, but through the eyes of the One who created you to flourish. He is faithful. He has begun a good work in you, and He will bring it to glorious completion.

Call to Action

As you move forward from this chapter, don't just let this be something you read—let it become something you live. Every promise you've encountered, every truth you've embraced, every testimony you've resonated with is meant to be walked out in your daily life. So, take time to get alone with God and ask, "Holy Spirit, show me what You've started in me. Teach me how to live from this place of love."

Look into the Word as a mirror—not to see what needs to be fixed, but to see who you already are in Christ. And when you see it, believe it. Declare it. Live it. Say no to fear. Say no to delay. Say no to the lie that you're not enough. And say yes to love. Say yes to identity. Say yes to flourishing. You were created for this. So, partner with the Spirit of God, walk boldly in your authority, and live today—fully and freely—as the loved, chosen, flourishing child of God you truly are.

And never forget—it is God's love that is in relentless pursuit of you. Not because you chased Him perfectly, but because He refused to give up on you. Every page of this book, every verse, every truth, has been about one thing: a Father who relentlessly loves you and refuses to let anything stand in the way of His goodness in your life. That's what changes everything. That's what transforms you. That's what causes you to flourish. His pursuit is not passive—it's powerful. And it is not over—it's only just beginning.

Scriptures Referenced

- Philippians 1:6
- Romans 8:30–31
- 2 Peter 1:3
- 2 Peter 1:4
- James 1:22–25
- Galatians 5:6
- Psalm 143:8

About the Author

Carrie Pickett has been a believer for over forty years and sensed God's call to be a missionary and Bible teacher from a young age. She has ministered in more than thirty-five nations and spent sixteen years as a full-time missionary in Russia after graduating from Charis Bible College. It was there that she met her husband, Mike Pickett, who was also serving as a missionary.

Together, Mike and Carrie launched and built Andrew Wommack Ministries and Charis Bible College across Russia, impacting sixteen Russian-speaking nations. They currently serve as the Executive Vice Presidents of Andrew Wommack Ministries and Charis Bible College International.

Carrie is the Director of the Woodland Park campus in Colorado and one of the primary instructors at Charis, equipping the next generation of ministers for global impact. She is also a visionary within the Gospel Truth Network, where she hosts the daily program *Life Foundations* and co-hosts *Andrew's Classics* alongside Andrew Wommack and her husband. In addition, she contributes to numerous other programs for the expanding global network.

Writing and developing new teaching materials to support conferences, leadership training, and worldwide outreach is a central passion of her ministry.

In the midst of her leadership and teaching roles, Carrie treasures her calling as a wife and mother. She and Mike travel extensively with their two children, who are growing up immersed in ministry and missions.

Contact Information

CarriePickett.com
719-635-1111
info@gtntv.com

Andrew Wommack Ministries, Inc.

PO Box 3333
Colorado Springs, CO 80934-3333
info@awmi.net
awmi.net

Helpline: 719-635-1111 (available 24/7)

Charis Bible College

info@charisbiblecollege.org
844-360-9577
CharisBibleCollege.org

For international offices,
visit **awmi.net/contact-us**.

Connect with us on social media.